Praise for *The Fight to Flourish*

"My wife didn't want to write this book. She was too busy living out its message—fighting to flourish. I am constantly amazed watching her go at it hammer and tongs, whether facing grief, our family life, or in our church as we pastor together. No, she didn't want to write this book, but that is precisely why it is so important that she did. This is no abstraction full of theories or poems you are about to read. *The Fight to Flourish* is a tear- and blood-stained playbook that has helped her face both victory and defeat with grace and grit, and it will help you do the same."

—Levi Lusko
Jennie's husband

"Each one of us eventually comes to a point in life when we are feeling weak and broken and don't know where to turn. We desperately need to hear a voice of truth speaking life to us in those times. Thankfully, Jennie Lusko steps up to be that voice for us in *The Fight to Flourish*. Jennie has walked through the valley in her own life and is a friend who has certainly strengthened me with words of hard-fought hope. In this book you'll treasure, she will help you press in and press on to live a life that looks a whole lot more like flourishing than it ever did before."

—Lysa TerKeurst
#1 *New York Times* bestselling author
President of Proverbs 31 Ministries

"Jennie and her husband, Levi, have been part of our extended family for a few years now. Their story of courage and perseverance in the midst of loss is inspiring, to say the least. I am confident that Jennie's story, perspective, and wisdom will bless multitudes. Life does have its shadowlands, yet there is always hope. I believe that *The Fight to Flourish* will be hope in darkness and hope in the journey for many."

—Bobbie Houston
Co-global senior pastor, Hillsong Church

"Jennie Lusko is a woman whose life reflects the miracle-ground forged when grace and resilience hold hands. The harvest coming from that ground—tilled, broken, planted, and watered in seasons of real, hard life—is something beautiful to behold and utterly God-glorifying. As you lean into the tested and lived-out lessons from this book, may hope and grit rise up in you as the Lord deposits courage in you for your own fight to flourish."

—Brooke Ligertwood
Head of Hillsong Worship

"Sometimes God knits friends into family. It's extraordinary, really, and we treasure having Jennie Lusko and her family as our people. Jennie's book, *The Fight to Flourish*, is a brave and faith-filled story of how to fight forward toward the flourishing version of yourself that God created you to be. Jennie, filled with sweetness and boldness, allows God to move powerfully in the midst of devastation and chooses to author a story that loudly echoes His glory. Way to go, Jennie. We love you."

—Shelley Giglio
Cofounder of Passion Conferences and Passion City Church

"Jennie Lusko embodies this message of flourishing unlike anyone else I know. Her life has blossomed, not just in spite of her great struggles but right through them. Jennie invites us into these transformational lessons learned with hard-won wisdom and supernatural grace. This book is a priceless guide for any hurting heart longing for more."

—Katherine Wolf
Author of *Suffer Strong* and *Hope Heals*

"We've all experienced some type of heartbreaking loss that only God Himself can lead us through. That's why Jennie's book is so necessary. She beautifully shares how, even when life isn't what you imagined it would be or should be, it is possible, through God's love and tender care, to take flight once again. If you're feeling weary, exhausted, busy, or if you're carrying a weight too great to bear, this book will show you the way."

—Roma Downey
Emmy-nominated actress, producer, and
New York Times bestselling author

"God has plans for each of us that far exceed anything we could ever ask, think, or imagine. *The Fight to Flourish* will encourage you to hold on to God's promise of an 'exceedingly abundantly more' life, even when yours feels completely out of reach."

—Christine Caine
Bestselling author
Founder of A21 & Propel Women

"The words in this book carry such honesty and offer true strength. Jennie so beautifully shares how you can thrive in the middle of those things you never expected would become part of your life. If you are ready to shed your burdens and step into a flourishing life, read this book. It will bring a freedom you never knew was possible."

—Alex Seeley
Lead pastor of The Belonging Co

"Maybe you feel like you're in a losing battle and have hit the ground too many times to count. Jennie Lusko has been there! Ready to discover the ongoing strength she found? Jennie wrote *The Fight to Flourish* as a charge to reengage life with renewed vision and confidence."

—Amy Groeschel
Cofounder of Life.Church, author, and founder of Branch15

"Everyone has a desire to flourish. To thrive and be successful. However, no one is exempt from the sting of pain. There's a decision between the place of pain and promise: to fight forward or to remain discouraged. This book speaks to that place. And I can think of no one better to speak to that place than Jennie. She is the fiercest fighter I know! I believe this book will equip you for the life you are called to live."

—Julia Veach
Lead pastor of ZOE Church LA

"We all want to flourish, but few are willing to fight for it. Through Jennie's powerful words and real-life experiences, she walks us through the work that is required to revive our roots to blossom and bloom. The teaching is profound, but her life lives a greater story. I believe this book this book will pour Living Water onto dry ground."

—Bianca Juarez Olthoff
Church planter, teacher, and bestselling author of
Play with Fire and *How to Have Your Life Not Suck*

"Jennie Lusko's faith cannot be ignored. It is raw and real. Both bold and beautiful, her faith shines more brightly through her sorrows than her successes. The untimely loss of her daughter Lenya thrust Jennie into the public spotlight, making her internal agony a grief observed. In this gut-wrenchingly honest book, Jennie lets us watch her mother's heart ache and break, and then witness God remake it into a sacred place of worship."

—Lenya Heitzig
Author and speaker

"As Greg and I have personally experienced, life doesn't always turn out like you had planned. It didn't for us when, in 2008, our son Christopher was suddenly called to heaven. Levi and Jennie were there for us in ways that mattered most.

"In this book, Jennie shows us how one can not only survive but flourish in dark seasons of suffering. Jennie Lusko is not only a dear friend to our family but one of the most beautiful examples of a wise and godly woman with a strong message of hope."

—Cathe Laurie
Founder and executive director of Virtue for Women

"Jennie has so beautifully lead by example what it means to embrace the fight. This book will challenge you to get some grit to 'fight to keep fighting' and yet still remain sweet and pliable in the hands of the Father. It's a reminder that while anchoring your roots down deep to flourish can feel overwhelming, He is in the deep with you."

—April Carter
A close friend of Jennie's

THE
FIGHT
TO
Flourish

THE
FIGHT
TO
Flourish

*Engaging in the Struggle to
Cultivate the Life
You Were Born to Live*

JENNIE LUSKO

W PUBLISHING GROUP

AN IMPRINT OF THOMAS NELSON

Published in Nashville, Tennessee, by W Publishing, an imprint of Thomas Nelson.

Author is represented by the literary agency of The Fedd Agency, Inc., P.O. Box 341973, Austin, Texas 78734.

Thomas Nelson titles may be purchased in bulk for educational, business, fund-raising, or sales promotional use. For information, please e-mail SpecialMarkets@ThomasNelson.com.

Any Internet addresses, phone numbers, or company or product information printed in this book are offered as a resource and are not intended in any way to be or to imply an endorsement by Thomas Nelson, nor does Thomas Nelson vouch for the existence, content, or services of these sites, phone numbers, companies, or products beyond the life of this book.

Unless otherwise noted, Scripture quotations are taken from the New King James Version®. © 1982 by Thomas Nelson. Used by permission. All rights reserved.

Scripture quotations marked NIV are taken from the Holy Bible, New International Version®, NIV®. Copyright © 1973, 1978, 1984, 2011 by Biblica, Inc.® Used by permission of Zondervan. All rights reserved worldwide. www.zondervan.com. The "NIV" and "New International Version" are trademarks registered in the United States Patent and Trademark Office by Biblica, Inc.®

Scripture quotations marked TPT are from The Passion Translation®. Copyright © 2017, 2018 by Passion & Fire Ministries, Inc. Used by permission. All rights reserved. ThePassionTranslation.com.

Scripture quotations marked NLT are taken from the Holy Bible, New Living Translation. © 1996, 2004, 2015 by Tyndale House Foundation. Used by permission of Tyndale House Publishers, a Division of Tyndale House Ministires, Carol Stream, Illinois 60188. All rights reserved.

Scripture quotations marked ESV are taken from the ESV® Bible (The Holy Bible, English Standard Version®). Copyright © 2001 by Crossway, a publishing ministry of Good News Publishers. Used by permission. All rights reserved.

Scripture quotations marked CEV are taken from the Contemporary English Version. Copyright © 1991, 1992, 1995 by American Bible Society. Used by permission.

Scripture quotations marked THE MESSAGE are taken from The Message. Copyright © by Eugene H. Peterson 1993, 1994, 1995, 1996, 2000, 2001, 2002. Used by permission of Tyndale House Publishers, Inc.

Scripture quotations marked NIrV are taken from the Holy Bible, New International Reader's Version®, NIrV®. Copyright © 1995, 1996, 1998 Biblica, Inc.® Used by permission of Zondervan. All rights reserved worldwide. www.zondervan.com. The "NIrV" and "New International Reader's Version" are trademarks registered in the United States Patent and Trademark Office by Biblica, Inc.®

ISBN 978-0-7852-3214-8 (HC)
ISBN 978-0-7852-3233-9 (eBook)
ISBN 978-0-7852-3390-9 (ITPE)

Library of Congress Cataloging-in-Publication Data

Library of Congress Control Number: 2020932692

Printed in the United States of America

20 21 22 23 24 LSC 10 9 8 7 6 5 4 3 2 1

To my husband and best friend: Levi, you have seen every angle of my personal fight to flourish, and yet you're my biggest encourager. Thank you for reminding me to stick to the plan.

To my sweethearts—Alivia, Daisy, Clover, Lennox, and you, too, Lenya: You have helped me in my journey more than you know.

I sure do love you, sweet fam of mine.

Contents

Contents

Foreword

A few days before Christmas we heard the news: Levi and Jennie Lusko had lost their five-year-old daughter.

My husband, Steven, immediately called Levi. Their conversation was short, maybe ten minutes long. He listened to Levi retell what had happened, then he told him we were so sorry and that we were praying.

When he got off the phone, he handed me Jennie's number and said, "I told Levi you would call Jennie."

Panic. Why would he volunteer me for that? I didn't know what to say. I didn't know her that well. We had met only a few times. What do you say to a woman who has lost her child? How will she even go on from here?

So I did what any brave but nonconfrontational person would do: I texted her. I wrote something like this: "Hi, Jennie. This is Holly Furtick. Steven gave me your number. I am so, so sorry to hear about Lenya. Please know that I am praying for you and that I am going to be sending you scriptures here and there. No need to respond. I cannot imagine your pain. We love you guys."

I had no idea that text would be the beginning of a very special friendship. Over the past several years, Jennie has taught me how to fight when you have every excuse to give up. I have watched her fight for her marriage, her children, and herself. She could have turned inward, pushed everyone away, and succumbed to bitterness, and no one would have blamed her. But something in her decided to fight to live—and not just to live but to flourish. Somehow she tapped into an inner strength and continued to fight day after day, and sometimes moment after moment.

Jennie wasn't okay. She was far from okay. She was broken. But she leaned into her pain rather than avoiding it. And she allowed her brokenness to help her experience the presence of God like never before. There is nothing like watching your friend bravely face the darkest season of her life. In a way I've never seen before, Jennie leaned into her pain and then pushed through it.

Many times I've seen grief flood Jennie's eyes mid conversation. I remember one particular time we were in a green room at a church where both of our husbands were ministering. We were chatting and getting to know the people in the room when someone casually asked Jennie how many children she had. It's a common question, but it carries so much pain for her. Graciously, but with tears in her eyes and a smile on her face, Jennie replied, "I have three on earth and one in heaven."

Jennie doesn't avoid places where people might ask difficult questions. She is a woman who understands that, although her life will never be the same, she *can* thrive in this new place.

Pain and suffering are a common denominator in life. No one is exempt. This book is for anyone who is looking for a guide to help them navigate their pain. Jennie has earned the right to speak into your life. She teaches from experience. If she can fight through the most unimaginable pain, so can you. The stories that Jennie recounts in this book are raw and honest, and I'm confident they will give you the handles you need to face your own situations.

Lenya's life here on earth was tragically cut short, but she lives on through the pages of this book. And I believe she is looking down from heaven proud of her momma who had the courage to fight and the fortitude to write down her story for all of us.

—Holly Furtick
Elevation Church, Charlotte, NC

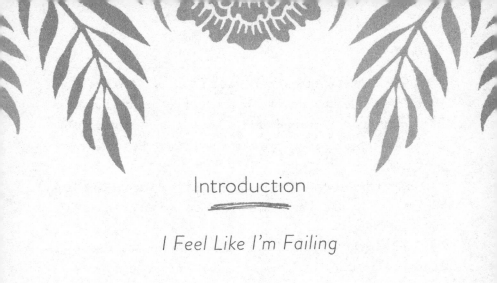

Introduction

I Feel Like I'm Failing

It's been six days since our five-year-old daughter, Lenya, died without warning. Six days since I snuggled her close. Six days since I heard the sound of her raspy voice.

The hundred-year-old theater is filled with row after row of people we love, but I don't remember seeing anyone's face. More occupy every inch of standing room. They gather with our family to celebrate the life of our little girl.

As musicians take the stage, the movement and whispers of the crowd dull. Guitars strum melodies honoring the Giver of life as the voices on stage blend with the crowd's, creating a beautiful harmony. I hold my husband's hand. The other I raise in worship, my heart riding the swells of awe and sadness, gratitude and loss.

As the music tapers, the moment comes for my husband, Levi, and I to walk on stage with our seven-year-old daughter. Levi briefly introduces Alivia, who opens her iPad and begins to share about her best friend and sister. Her words (which were well thought out, then written, and then typed) prompt tears.

Then, it's my turn. Heart racing, I try to catch my breath.

Truthfully, I don't want to say anything. I don't even feel like being there, let alone lending my voice to pour out my heart to hundreds of people through a microphone. That's my husband's job. He's the pastor, he's the professional preacher and teacher who speaks every week, not me.

Today I have the privilege of standing on that stage, celebrating the life of Lenya and sharing about my God, whom I don't understand but whom I trust.

Knees buckling, I lift the microphone to my lips. No words come. Instead, tears fall. To try and stop them is pointless.

There's no way I can do this. Who can blame me? Surely no one expects me to say anything anyway.

But there's something in me telling me I can. And I should. And how can I not? Levi whispers into my ear, "The same Holy Spirit who raised Jesus from the dead is in you. You can do this."

Fighting back the tears and the instinct to run away, I fill my lungs with oxygen, and as I exhale, my balance steadies. Words begin to flow as I share how I loved being Lenya's mom.

This was one of the first times I remember fighting against my feelings. I didn't want to get on stage and talk that day, but I knew I needed to give my heart a voice. Not just for the people with us but for my sake. I needed to make known my walk in the valley of the shadow of death and declare that God was there—and that He was good. It was in the grief that I learned to fight forward and to fight through. Little did I know that the fight would continue. And little did I know that the fight was what I needed to flourish.

My fight to flourish has stretched beyond the loss of my child.

It has become the everyday struggles for patience, passion, purpose, and peace.

The truth is, I usually feel like I'm failing in some way every day. I see who I want to be: The happy, sweet, sexy, laughing-out-loud kind of wife. The tender, confident, fun, strong mom. The thoughtful, wise, present sister and friend. This is the best version of me, the one who thrives in all she does. She also seems unattainable, out of reach, and it's so discouraging. How can I grow when I don't feel like I'm growing? How can I succeed when I'm facing a struggle of some kind every day, whether I'm late to another appointment or losing my temper with my kids?

I used to think *flourish* was a word that would never describe me—not until heaven anyway. And then I learned something that totally shifted my perspective. The word *flourish* in Hebrew is *parach*, which means "to revive, blossom; to sprout, shoot; become apparent, break out." The Greek version of this word, *anathallo*, is used only one time in the New Testament, when Paul said, "I rejoiced in the Lord greatly that now at last your care for me has flourished again; though you surely did care, but you lacked opportunity" (Philippians 4:10). You may have known that verse to say "revived" instead of "flourished" if you've read it in a different translation. This is the essence of the same word in Hebrew, to return to a former state of being.

And here is where we learn that the word *flourish* is pretty spectacular. When God calls us to flourish, it doesn't mean to become something brand new. It means to revive, to bring back to life what and who we were meant to be. We weren't created to become something totally different but to become what we were originally designed for.

I love how most grocery stores sell plants and flowers. Makes it easy to pick up butter, broccoli, Taco Tuesday ingredients, and a happy house plant all in one trip. If you walk into a home improvement store, you won't find guacamole, but you'll find a huge department that exists to provide everything you could possibly need to start your own garden: gnome statues, wind chimes, watering cans, potted plants, flowers, and packets with seeds so you can grow your own plants, trees, flowers, herbs, fruits, and vegetables. How do you know what kind of seed is in each packet? Easy—there's a picture on it.

You gently open the packet, careful not to lose any seeds, and look at these tiny, generally not pretty, seemingly insignificant specks. It doesn't seem possible that these puny seeds will grow into the beautiful picture of the sunflower or the zinnia portrayed on the outside. No way. Can't happen. Yet somehow, it does.

The picture of the fully grown, lush specimen of botany is what you are meant to become. It's you. But you're also the seed. It's you too.

God sees you as that picture. You're not quite there, yet you are already there. Confusing? I know. It's a spiritual paradox. But wait—there's more.

The picture on your packet is the true version of you. And the only way to become the version of you that you were born to be is to be found in Jesus Christ. The picture is actually of Jesus.

Romans 8:29 says, "For he knew all about us before we were born and he destined us from the beginning to share the likeness of his Son. This means the Son is the oldest among a vast family of brothers and sisters who will become just like him" (TPT).

You are made in the image of God, in the image of His Son. Do you know that in Christ you are perfect? When God looks at you, He sees Jesus—and Jesus is the picture of what it means to flourish.

The Bible teaches us that when we surrender to Jesus, we are, in a moment, made righteous. We don't earn salvation; we believe and receive freely. We don't pay for it—not with money, not with the good things we do. It's purely a gift from the God who loves us. We're covered by the grace found only in Jesus through His death and resurrection. And in that moment of salvation, we're made like Christ. So when God looks at us, He sees Jesus. That doesn't seem possible to me, but it's the way God does it, and it's beautiful.

But until we get to heaven, where we will truly be perfect like Jesus, we're still here, in these imperfect bodies and minds. We're in a period of sanctification. That's a fancy way of saying that, yes, we're already in Christ, and yes, we're also still in the process of becoming more like him—right now. We're living in the dash between the date of our birth and the date of our last breath on earth. That last breath will lead us to our first breath in heaven with Jesus. But we're not there yet.

Does flourishing in this life seem out of reach? It often feels like that to me. I often feel an underlying sense of guilt because I'm not measuring up and I'm not where I thought I would be. If only there wasn't such a struggle in my soul. The great news, though, is that we are actually in the process of flourishing right now, whether we feel it or not.

A seed is destined to become a mature plant, but it requires the right soil, water, air, light, and temperature. In this book I want to help you understand that a fight "breaks out" (*parach*) when the seed hits the soil. It's not just go time; it's grow time. And that means it's time to fight.

I suspect that you can understand the reality of the fight through the filter of your own story. I love what 1 Timothy 6:12 tells us: "Fight the good fight of the faith. Take hold of the eternal life to which you were called when you made your good confession in the presence of many witnesses" (NIV). This word *fight* in the Greek language (in which the New Testament was written) is *agonizomai*, and it means "to fight, to contend, to strive as in a contest for a prize." We see a tension here between faith, receiving the gift of salvation given by God, and the action of fighting and taking hold of the life we were born to live. We receive freely, and we also act vigorously.

The author gives us a real-life picture of fighting the good fight of faith with everything we've got, to strain to obtain the prize. This resonates in my heart because two of my favorite things are boxing and spin class. Do I love punishment? No, but if I need to stay healthy by exercising, then I want to at least have some fun while doing it.

These workouts show me what I have in me. I can do more than I think I can. I can push myself a little more than it may seem. I can work really hard, and then see the results—getting stronger and gaining endurance. I realize not everyone loves to exercise, but if you stick with me, I want to show you some of the truths I've extracted from pushing myself physically. I hope to help you see that you indeed have grit. And that you can grow it. You also have the stamina and endurance to grow stronger in whatever you are facing right now, good or bad. I want you to see that you can fight, that you can grow, that you can be fruitful, and that you can flourish.

You may feel as though you're not flourishing *because* of the fight, *because* of the struggle. But it's the embracing of the fight that will create the space to flourish. A fight for honor. A fight for a sweet spirit. A fight to choose to get uncomfortable. A fight to keep fighting. Jesus said, "These things I have spoken to you, that in Me you may have peace. In the world you will have tribulation; but be of good cheer, I have overcome the world" (John 16:33). Jesus doesn't mention overcoming the trouble; He tells us He has overcome the world. We want Him to take away the trial, but He's taking care of the even bigger picture: the world our trouble is in.

I once went out on a limb and started a garden. Keep in mind, it was a tiny one, about two feet by four feet. I envisioned the kids picking strawberries for their yogurt and granola every morning, and me collecting tiny leaves of parsley and mint to flavor sauce and salads. From my backyard to my table—that was my dream.

It was a good little garden, for a brief moment. Things grew— and then they didn't. Or they died before they could thrive. Bless the little garden's heart; it barely provided the things I wanted most. The strawberries were tiny and the herbs were few. It had grown, but it had not flourished.

God doesn't want us to barely peek through the hard soil of life like a tiny weed or a puny bunch of strawberries. He wants us to shoot through the dirt and grow into a tree with deep roots, a thick trunk, strong branches, and most of all, fruit. He wants us to grow luxuriantly. How do I know this? He told us clearly in Psalm 92:

> The righteous will flourish like a palm tree,
> they will grow like a cedar in Lebanon;
> planted in the house of the LORD,
> they will flourish in the courts of our God.
> They will still bear fruit in old age,
> they will stay fresh and green,
> proclaiming, "The LORD is upright;
> he is my Rock, and there is no wickedness in him."
> (vv. 12–15 NIV)

The progression of action in this psalm could be wrapped up like this: God plants, God waters, we receive, and we flourish.

Palm trees know how to stand their ground. They can grow as tall as two hundred feet and can endure tropical storms. Palm trees may bend, but they will not break. Their roots grow even deeper over time. They may take years to grow, but they last for centuries. They produce sweet fruit like acai, coconuts, and dates.

Cedars can grow to be 130 feet tall with a trunk diameter of over 8 feet. The ancient cedars of Lebanon have existed for thousands of years, surviving wars and storms, even outlasting empires. Because of their high-quality, incorruptible timber, these trees were the first-choice material used to build temples and palaces.

Cedars flourish in cold mountain climates, the kind that my family and I live in now in northwest Montana. I am always amazed how the trees—especially the deciduous ones, the ones that lose their leaves—stay alive in the winter. When autumn sighs to a close and the trees are done showing off their most beautiful and brightest colors, it looks like they die. There's no life left in their empty branches—or so it seems. But what's really happening is dormancy. The trees are in a period of rest. The life source within them focuses its energy on keeping the trees alive during the brutal winter months.

Much like the growth of these legendary trees, we, too, are meant to fight to grow and to bloom. To push through our small and seemingly insignificant seedlike stages. To persevere through the dirt and mess, through the growth and beauty. To experience the strength to live the life that God has designed for us, that He can see even if we can't.

Someone recently asked me if I'm a green thumb, and I replied that I'm more of a green eye. I don't grow things very successfully, but I know a happy house plant when I see one. I just love greenery and plants and trees, and I'm a botanist at heart. I don't know every-thing about botany, but I do know that seeds don't all grow and bloom at the same rate and at the same time. A palm tree takes four to six years to fully mature, but a cedar can take multiple decades. The queen of the Andes, a rare forty-foot plant that thrives in harsh climates, flowers just once and only for a few weeks in its eighty-to one-hundred-year lifetime. There are seeds that even need strange elements to germinate, like some Australian plants that require the heat of fire.

And just like seeds germinate and mature at different rates, we each flourish in our own way and in our own time. There's no room for comparison. We are each running or walking or even speed walking in our own soil, at our own pace, in our own seasons, with our own unique DNA. I don't have to have the same stride as you. You have a different stride from me. And that's okay.

I recently hiked a mountain with my friends. At the start of the hike, there were two trails to choose from. One was lush and green and dotted with flowers. Birds sang in the trees lining the trail, inviting me forward. I was about to happily turn that way and enjoy a picturesque hike with my friends, but they said, "Oh Jennie, we're actually going *this* way!"

I turned toward the trail they pointed to. Horror met my eyes in the form of the steepest incline I'd ever seen. I couldn't see the top, just up. And then *more* up. There were no trees. Nothing lush. Barely any flowers. I couldn't hear any birds—or anything else, except possibly the soundtrack to the scariest movie you've ever seen playing faintly in the background.

It was the hardest hike of my life (although it wasn't the hardest of the hikes on this mountain by a long shot). As I climbed, I felt as if I was barely making any forward progress. I may have been slower than my friends, but I made it (with the help and encouragement of one of my friends taking it slow with me). I may have had to take more breaks than them, but I made it. I may have slipped back a few times, but I made it.

—

True flourishing comes from embracing the difficulty of growth. And we can't do that in our own strength. God doesn't call us to flourish, then pat us on the back and ditch us. He doesn't say, "Okay, Jennie, good luck, have fun! Don't wither and die out there!" God calls us and then equips us. He empowers us. He strengthens us for battle. And He is with us the whole way.

We just sent off our oldest daughter to public middle school after being homeschooled her whole life. While it was so hard to let her go, to drop her off at school that first day and watch her walk into the unknown, it was comforting to know we would pick her up at the end of the day and talk about how it went. We'd continue the conversation over dinner and later in the hot tub. We aren't sending Alivia off with "Good luck! Don't make bad choices. See you next year when you go to high school!" and neglecting to equip her. We are walking with her, training her, and teaching her the very best we can.

As you fight to flourish, my hope is that my words on the following pages will remind you that God is with you, teaching, training, and empowering you. The fighting you do now will lead you to the flourishing version of you God created you to be.

As I look back, I see how God was preparing my heart for the worst experience of my life. A few months before Lenya went to heaven, I was reading the book *In Search of Balance* by Richard Swenson. This line struck me: "We had better love with abandon, for what's around the corner is not ours to know."

True flourishing

comes from

embracing

the difficulty

of growth.

I'm so grateful that God, who is so good and loves me so much, would ready my heart for what was around the corner. He knew that 2012 would begin with celebrating the birth of our fourth child, Clover Dawn Lusko—and He knew it would end with mourning the death of our second-born daughter, Lenya Avery Lusko. God wasn't surprised by this. And He was in control all along.

I don't know what this year will bring you or what last year or the one before that did. I do know that God loves you, and that you can trust Him. Whatever fight you might be in today, know that you have the word *flourish* written all over you and your future.

I'm so grateful you have decided to join me in this journey. As we walk together, I want you to see how special you are and that where you are in life right now is special. I want you to know that it's not only possible for you to flourish in the middle of this fight but that it's necessary to have this fight in order to flourish. I'm in this with you, and I hope in sharing some of my struggles, you can see how you can keep growing.

If you find yourself asking the question "How can I flourish in this season?" I want to help you see that it's not just dirt you're planted in; it's soil with the right nutrients. It's not just crap you feel stuck in; it's the fertilizer you need. You're not buried with no way out; you're planted. You're not taking a lifetime to bloom on the outside; you're growing a strong and deep root system under the surface. You're not forgotten; you've been sown by a Gardener who fights for you.

Let's grow, girl.

1

The Best, the Worst, and the In Between

Fighting forward often doesn't feel like it—forward, that is. It feels more like survival. Barely getting by. Dripping in sweat, muscles aching, legs failing, but still standing, at least long enough so that your opponent doesn't take you down with a one-two punch before the bell rings.

Doesn't sound much like flourishing.

Hard times have a way of knocking us off our feet, but they also have a way of reminding us of what is most important. Before the worst day of my life, I loved God and I trusted Him. I knew that heaven was real and near, and I knew God had a purpose for me. But in the year Lenya died, God had been teaching me so much, not only about Him but about myself. In fact, I remember so clearly feeling like I was learning more in that year than I had in my whole life. It was a season of growth. I had four daughters, six years old and under. I was being stretched and strengthened in my heart, in my family, in our church. I had no idea that God had even more for me as 2012 drew to a close, no idea that I would feel His presence more than ever, even in darkness.

Reliving Lenya's life and last days on earth in order to share this story with you has been one of the hardest things I have ever done. Flipping through journal entries splashed with tears; replaying scenes of our daughter dancing, reciting Bible verses, and playing with her sisters; remembering what she looked like when her body had surrendered its last breath—these things gutted me. But they also gave me the chance to connect some dots. Some of the most random moments in this story have been the most important. They're reminders that God is in control behind the scenes, reminders that He was, is, and will always be with me.

Words of Life

It was Thursday morning, six days before Christmas 2012. Fresh coffee brewed as eggs sizzled in the frying pan. Daisy looked at a book as if she were reading, although she was only two and she couldn't read (or could she?). Clover giggled in her high chair, observing everything like a tiny queen on her throne. As Alivia dressed for the day, I heard a cadence of footsteps coming down the stairs that could only be Lenya's. Her feet landed a bit harder and louder than the others. It was morning as usual in the Lusko household.

I scrambled eggs as Lenya settled at the table, her thick, messy hair tumbling over her head as she scribbled a birthday note for a friend's party in a few hours. I looked at her outfit and smiled. She wore one of Alivia's sparkly shirts paired with denim bell-bottoms a size too big for her with her favorite skirt over them, and hand-me-down boots from a friend. Around her neck hung one of my necklaces adorned with plastic beads in the shape of birds. It was a wild outfit—Lenya style to the max.

The week was full of dinners, meetings, staff events, and birthday parties. I was exhausted, and I reminded myself that although things might be crazy now, Friday Family Day was coming. And it was going to be the best.

Friday is Levi's and my day off. We unplug from everything to spend time as a family with as few distractions as possible. We had plans to swish and stumble our way around a rink with ice skates strapped to our feet. Levi would take Lenya to shop for presents for her sisters, and afterward we would all dress up and enjoy a fancy dinner out.

But first we had to make it through Thursday. After the kids finished their eggs and oatmeal and I plucked an unknown object off Clover's face and wiped up a sticky substance on the counter, we scrambled out the door to the eventful day ahead.

"Wait!" Lenya shouted, almost falling forward as she stopped in the doorway. "I have to write a Christmas card to Aunt Aimee!" Another delay, but I knew how important this was for her. I gave her the time to write the note, and we left it on the table to mail later. Lenya was thoughtful like that. In her five-year-old mind and tender heart, she knew the power of words, that they could bring a smile to someone's face, brighten a dull mood, or turn tears into laughter.

I love words. I don't have a widely extensive vocabulary myself, and I usually stumble to find the words I'm looking for in conversation, but I am fascinated by them, what they mean, and where they originate from. God loves words so much that He filled a book with them. Not only that, but He gave us the Word of all words, as it says in John 1:1–5:

> In the beginning was the Word, and the Word was with God, and the Word was God. He was in the beginning with God. All

things were made through Him, and without Him nothing was made that was made. In Him was life, and the life was the light of men. And the light shines in the darkness, and the darkness did not comprehend it.

Jesus is the Word, and He changes everything. God's words in the Bible can transform our hearts and our lives. In the same way, the words people speak over us can give us the strength we need in the fight.

A little over a week earlier, Levi and I had strolled through the congested sidewalks of New York City. With my arm linked through his, we drank in the holiday window displays on Fifth Avenue and shopped for a few extra Christmas gifts for the girls. I even bought a pair of dusty-rose corduroys for myself. They weren't something I would normally wear, but I tend to shop impulsively like that.

We had talked about seeing a Broadway play that night, but instead we found ourselves at a midweek worship gathering hosted by our friends. The church met in an old theater with a large stage and ornate ceiling and walls. It was dark, yet inviting. I felt the beat and the bass in the music deep in my chest.

The room filled with expectation and anticipation as a pastor I didn't know started encouraging specific people in the room. I don't know about you, but I had never experienced anything like this growing up. I had heard of churches where the pastor takes a moment to listen to what God might be speaking to specific people in a packed room. I imagined it could get a little awkward; people are sitting there, not knowing if they should stick around or use a restroom break as an excuse to run away. But there was nothing awkward about what happened to me.

As the pastor spoke inspiring and challenging words to different people in the room, I rummaged around my giant mom bag. My fingers frantically pushed aside my hand sanitizer, allergy medicine, a diaper, in search of tissues for the woman next to me, who was moved to tears. *Why on earth did I bring this thing with me when my kids aren't even here?*

As I placed my purse back on the floor underneath my seat, I heard the pastor call my name.

I froze. *Wait. Did he just say my name? He must certainly mean Levi, not me. Or maybe he means another, more significant Jennie. Probably a Jennie who spells her name with a y at the end.* My heart began to beat wildly. *What is he going to tell me? Is he going to call me out on something in front of everyone?*

"Jen—Jennie," he began, his voice powerful and comforting at the same time.

"It is not an accident you are here, Jennie . . . You didn't know you were going to be here. I don't think that was the big plan. I don't know; maybe it was. Jennie, you are going to walk away with a new impartation tonight. God has placed something into your heart. I don't know you from a bar of soap, but you have a new authority about you . . . God is going to challenge you to take a risk in Him, to trust Him, to believe that He is with you. He's going to back you, Jennie. His heart is toward you. His face is toward you. His hand is toward you. You mustn't ever forget that. You are blessed, Jennie, not cursed. God's hand is on you. You are here in the purpose and plan of God."

This was so out of the ordinary. I didn't really know what to do with his message. Tears filled my eyes and fell freely down my face.

What happened in that theater that evening was a holy moment. I may have not understood it fully, but something beautiful unfolded when that man's words hit my heart. It's always amazing to be reminded that we are not alone, that God is with us, and that He loves us. I thought about these things as we made our way back home the next day.

The following week, thrust into the chaos of preparing for Christmas and scuttling through a calendar full to the brim with nonstop events and growing lists, I wrote about my experience in my journal:

> This has been such a busy season. Nonstop. Like literally. But I'm not freaking out and it's only by God's grace. I've had to speak in front of people three times in three days, and tonight Levi and I are doing a capture together for the recap of what we learned this year. And it's really not easy for me—I get so nervous, but I've been really taking God at His word when He told me to be bold and to speak confidently because God is my backing. He only is my strength. And I've been experiencing this. It's been a week today since Pastor Robert spoke that over me, and I've had more opportunities in these last four days than in a long time. . . . I truly believe that this year has been a huge year for me. I fully believe that I have grown more in 2012 than in my whole life combined!
>
> Life is good!

When the Best Turns into the Worst

On Thursday afternoon, I dropped the kids off at my mom's for the evening so Levi and I could have an at-home date night (a practice I highly recommend). I could wrap the kids' presents without them peeking or grabbing my scissors or chewing on the gift tags, and my mom would get to spend time with her grandkids. Win-win. After enjoying my specialty—spaghetti with meat sauce—and quality make-out time with my husband, I buried myself in gifts and tape and ribbons and paper, while Levi watched *Home Alone*. As I finished putting the creative touch on the last gift, I remember soaking in the moment, grateful for time spent together before the start of our wildly wonderful Family Day.

On the drive to my mom's to pick up the kids, Levi sighed loudly, exhaling away the past few days. "I just feel so relaxed."

I nodded, rubbing his forearm draped over my thigh. I felt the same. Friday was here—well, almost, but basically here. Heat blasted from the vents. Outside, stars sprinkled the midnight Montana sky over a landscape of glistening snow. White. Pure. Bright. Light in the darkness.

And then, though we'd barely pulled into my mom's driveway, silence traded spaces with panic. My younger brother, David, ran out the front door, and as I met him at the edge of the walkway, he blurted, "Jennie, Lenya really wants you!" His breath was ragged. "She's not taking her asthma treatment!"

My heart plunged to the pit of my stomach. Sprinting into the kitchen, I found Lenya sitting on the table. My mom was holding her. Lenya looked at me, her face blank and drained of color.

I grabbed the nebulizer from my mom, held Lenya with one arm, and tried to get her to take her treatment. Instead, she passed out. Even today, the image of her lying limp on the kitchen counter tears me apart.

At that moment, Levi came in the house and immediately jumped into action. His hands clamped down rhythmically on Lenya's tiny chest, but there was no response. Time began to churn in slow motion, but in a blur. I remember crying desperate prayers toward heaven and telling Lenya that I loved her and that it was going to be okay. Because it was, right?

Lights and sirens filled the driveway as paramedics rushed in and rushed our little girl back out on a stretcher. Levi rode with her. My brother drove me in my car on the icy road a few minutes behind the ambulance.

As Levi and I waited in a small room at the hospital, crying and praying, a doctor appeared.

I wanted to believe the best, I wanted to hope for the miracle, but in my gut, I knew Lenya was gone. She had stopped breathing so long ago.

"I am so sorry, Mr. and Mrs. Lusko. Lenya is nonresponsive. There is nothing more we can do."

It was as if I couldn't really hear the words coming from his mouth. I knew what he was saying, but I can only remember things happening in slow motion as he began to speak. His words, slowly connecting to my mind, were words of death. It was actually true: our five-year-old was gone.

We followed him to a room where Lenya lay. And here is where heaven truly met earth, where the tension between light and darkness collided in a way I had never before experienced. It felt as though someone had come up behind us and pushed us into a pit with only one way in and no way out. And at the same time, as I stepped toward our daughter's body, I couldn't help but feel that even in my darkest night I was overwhelmed by the love of the Light of the world.

It is unnatural to look at your child when her soul has left this earth. That second, my heart began a slow and steady break that would, over time, morph into a permanent dull ache. Lenya's eyes were open. Her face was cool to my touch, her features beautiful and delicate. Levi took one of her hands, and I held the other on the opposite side of the stretcher.

"God, You give and take away. Blessed be Your name. You gave us Lenya. We don't understand, but we give her back to You." Levi's words were words of surrender and praise spoken with our daughter lying lifeless before us. Words wrapped in a peace beyond what the human mind can comprehend. We felt God with us as tears streamed from our eyes and Levi reached down to close hers.

While my worst day was unfolding one terrible scene at a time, I realized an awful yet beautiful tension. Our worst day was actually Lenya's best day. Her death, while horrible to us, led her straight to her Savior. The Bible says that to be absent from the body is to be present with the Lord (2 Corinthians 5:8). She wasn't with us, but she was with Jesus. Lenya was in heaven, more alive now than she had ever been.

How Am I Supposed to Leave the Hospital?

In that room, my protective mama heart swarmed with questions. We had worked so hard to take care of Lenya, to make sure she was healthy and loved. Suddenly she had been snatched away from us into heaven, a place that seems so big, crowded, and overwhelming—a place so far away from our arms. I wondered who was taking care of her. Was she wandering around all by herself? Was anyone assigned to watch her? Was she lost?

My mind spun in every direction. I'll never forget looking down and noticing my pants, the pink corduroy ones I bought in New York City. As my gaze rested on the stunning face of our daughter, the words spoken to me eight days earlier echoed softly: *You are*

I didn't have

to understand

God in order

to trust Him.

blessed, not cursed. You are in the plan and purpose of God. His hand is on you. His face is toward you. God has your back.

I knew these were scriptural truths. But I also knew that Lenya was dead and wouldn't be coming back. It's hard to reconcile the two, but deep down in my heart, I knew I didn't have to understand God in order to trust Him.

Trusting God came instinctively in that moment, but there were other fights I would still have to show up for—the first one being, how was I supposed to leave the hospital?

I honestly don't know how long we were there. I know Alivia came in at one point bringing Lenya's purse with her, and we had to tell her that her sister was in heaven. But eventually, I found myself in the front seat of our car. I don't remember how I got there, though I do remember suggesting to Levi that we invite everyone at the ER that night to church.

How did I move forward? Step by dreaded step, walking toward a new reality that I despised. Weeping. Reminding myself that the body of my daughter I left in that unnaturally bright and cold hospital room wasn't all she was. Yes, her body was there, but her soul—who she really was—was with her Savior in heaven. She was perfectly pure in His presence.

I had to make the intentional decision to walk out the front door. And I had to choose to trust God in the middle of the pain. I knew I couldn't face a single thing without Him as my guide, as my lamp lighting the road before me. I couldn't do anything in my own strength.

I wish I could tell you I've arrived and that I have a five-step program for how to leave the hospital, so to speak. I haven't, and I don't. I fight every day. It's a fight to love. A fight to grow. But I want to fight to flourish. Like the seed surrounded by darkness and dirt, we need these very elements to grow. It's what we need to become stronger.

In January 2013, sixteen days after Lenya went to heaven, I bought a new journal, an extra-large, plain black notebook. Unmarked, unlined pages begged to absorb new thoughts, new memories, new insight. I titled it *A New Chapter. A Terrible One. A Beautiful One.*

Therefore we do not lose heart. Even though our outward man is perishing, yet the inward man is being renewed day by day. For our light affliction, which is but for a moment, is working for us a far more exceeding and eternal weight of glory, while we do not look at the things which are seen, but at the things which are not seen. For the things which are seen are temporary, but the things which are not seen are eternal. (2 Corinthians 4:16–18)

As I look ahead to this year, I have so many emotions/ thoughts/feelings/fears. I hate the thought of approaching this year without Lenya. I love the thought that she is in His presence in fullness of joy. I hate the thought of the possibility of forgetting memories with her / of her. I love that I got five wonderful years with her. I hate those demonic thoughts of regret and how I should've been a better mommy to her. I love that talk of heaven was always on our lips—that we talked about Jesus + His Word + prayed always. I love that we had a full five years with her. I hate that she's not here anymore. I love Lenya. I hate that our lives are forever changed. I love that we have three beautiful daughters to teach and to train and to love. I hate this aching in my soul. At the same time, I love it because I've never experienced God like this before → His grace → His love → His peace. I'm floored. This light affliction is for a moment. This year I cling to Jesus. I cling to His word. I stand on His promises. I choose to do right. I choose to worship and obey.

When we're shoved into a storm, it can be easy to flounder. What growth is even possible when we're doing everything we can just to keep our heads above water? But it is possible to see God's goodness in the struggle, His love over the valley of death, His grace through the pain. I hold tight to the hope of heaven, yet I also grieve. I hurt. I love. I cry. I remember. I feel stuck. I move forward. It's in this tension that we can grow, if we keep trusting God and believing He is with us and has more for us.

Sunshine at the Grave

Years later, I stand in a cemetery on a cloudy day. Headstones stretch as far as the eye can see. I don't come here very often; I know Lenya's not here. But when I do stand at her grave, I am reminded of eternity. On her headstone, we chose to write 2 Timothy 1:10: "Christ Jesus, who has destroyed death and has brought life and immortality to light through the gospel" (NIV).

The air freezes my face. I can barely feel the falling tears. I'm reminded that the body of the little girl I carried in my womb, birthed in a room with a view of Glacier National Park, nurtured through medical struggles, and snuggled tight, lies underneath the cold ground. My heart aches in the deepest parts, a pain too great to carry.

I have to remind myself I'm not alone. I don't have to carry this heavy weight by myself. I wasn't meant to. Psalm 68:19 says, "Praise be to the Lord, to God our Savior, who daily bears our burdens"

I don't have

to pull myself

together to

run to Him.

(NIV). God is with me. And He doesn't only carry the things that weigh me down; He also carries me.

I worship as I weep. The cloudy day depicts the state of my heart: gray. I'm so thankful I don't need sunshine in my heart in order to worship Jesus. I don't have to pull myself together to run to Him. I can be who I am, right where I am, with Him.

As I ache and long for heaven, the clouds part, inviting in a ray of sunlight that seems meant just for me: a picture of God reminding me of His presence in an overcast moment.

As pastor Robert Ferguson told me that night in New York City, maybe you didn't plan to be here in this place, in this pain, in this predicament, or even on this platform, but it's not an accident. God has called you uniquely for this situation, right here, right now. Whatever you are facing as you read these words, my hope is for you to be confident that you were born for this very fight. And you were born to flourish in it.

2

Born to Shine

When we're in the middle of the struggle, it can be easy to miss the beauty in it. The pain we feel can make us blind to the growth that's happening under the surface. The frustration with the fight can keep us preoccupied with the tiny sprouts of growth that aren't even visible to the naked eye. Pain can paralyze our vision and shame can stunt our growth. But there's actually something beautiful hidden beneath the dirt. There is a courage concealed, a strength simmering, and a wisdom waiting to be seen.

After Lenya went to heaven, there were tiny little glimpses of beauty that I would see every now and then as the waves of grief tumbled over and around me. Like the people who emerged from the woodwork of our lives, who showed up and stuck around to support us and be strong for us. Or like the deeper heavenly perspective that instinctively struck us, locked into place, and overwhelmed us in the best way.

I think of how we were designed to appreciate beauty. We're drawn to works of art painted with intentionality and thought. We take in the intricate, creative designs of the storefront display of our favorite shops. We observe with wonder a mural on the side of a building and consider the artist's inspiration. We see a landscape of mountains and trees, or ocean and sand, and stare in amazement.

God made us beautiful and to be drawn to the beautiful. We were created not only to look for beauty but to live beautifully, to seek inspiration, and to live an inspiring life even when we don't feel like it.

The Bible begins with this:

In the beginning God created the heavens and the earth. Now the earth was formless and empty, darkness was over the surface of the deep, and the Spirit of God was hovering over the waters. And God said, "Let there be light," and there was light. God saw that the light was good, and he separated the light from the darkness. God called the light "day," and the darkness he called "night." And there was evening, and there was morning—the first day. (Genesis 1:1–5 NIV)

In the beginning God created. The Hebrew word for "create" in this passage is *bara*, which means "to shape, fashion (always with God as subject)." God is the OG fashion designer. He is the master of seeing the possibilities of a blank canvas. He is the ultimate scientist who can create something beautiful from absolutely nothing. And from this verse, it seems His specialty is creating light out of darkness.

Designed for Good

It was when I was a little girl that I first heard I was designed by God and created for good. I had the privilege of growing up in a church that taught the Bible and in a family that loved and followed Jesus. When I was seven years old, my dad prayed with me, and I made the decision to trust in Jesus and give Him my heart. As I entered middle school, I learned that I was special and worth waiting for. My youth pastor and his wife always encouraged me and reminded me that God had special plans for me, to give me a good future and a secure hope. So early on I understood that God loved me and created me for a purpose.

Whether or not you had someone speak these things over you, the truth is that God designed humans in a unique way. He designed *you* in a unique way. He fashioned us from the dust of the earth. At first glance, that may not seem super special. We're made from dirt? My husband recently preached a message about this very thing. Levi said, "God looked at the dirt and didn't just see dirt. He saw a home for His breath." A sophisticatedly designed human being made from dust? Now that's thinking creatively.

After creating the first human, God said that it was not good for him to be alone (Genesis 2:18). Everything God had made up until this point was good. But then, suddenly, it wasn't. The Hebrew word for "good" here is *tob*, which means "pleasant, agreeable, delightful." But man being alone was a problem—the first problem ever. The state of man on his own was not good. Nor was it pleasant. Or agreeable. Or delightful.

So God's creative solution was fashion. He *fashioned* a woman and brought her to the man. God gave women the unique role of making a not-good situation good. What a special calling that applies to each of us!

Proverbs 18:22 says, "He who finds a wife finds a good thing, and obtains favor from the LORD." A good thing. We were designed to bring good and to unlock favor in the lives of people around us. For those of us who are married, that includes our husbands, but whether you're a wife or not, God's highest potential is for you to be a good thing. You were created to make your surroundings, your situation, someone in your life better. You have a great superpower—to bring good. Whether or not you feel as though you're actively bringing good into the world, this is what God designed you for. If this is a struggle for you, as it is for me, then I want to encourage you that it's not too late to ask God to help you grow to be the good thing He created you to be.

You're meant to shine. The word *shine* means "to give forth or glow with light; shed or cast light; to be bright with reflected light; glisten, sparkle." I want the words *glisten* and *sparkle* to describe me! This reminds me of an incredible woman in the Bible named Esther.

In the Spotlight

Esther was a Jew who lived in Persia. Orphaned at a young age, she was raised by her cousin Mordecai. At the time, the king of Persia had made some bad decisions, had brought on some drama in his life, and in a drunken stupor, ended up kicking his wife, the queen, out of the palace and out of his life. Once he got lonely and started to regret his decision, the king's executive team arranged a beauty contest to find a new queen. Esther was one of many contestants. She was a normal girl, transformed and beautified to be presented before the king. And she won *Miss Congeniality* style—going from major makeover to wearing the crown. Esther became the queen of Persia overnight. While Esther was settling into her new role as queen, a man named Haman, who was in love with himself and with power, fought his way to the top as the king's right-hand man. Haman was offended by Esther's cousin and allowed that bitterness to drive him mad. He decided the only remedy for his hatred was to kill Esther's people, the Jews.

Esther is most famously known for her response when Mordecai strongly advised that she beg the king for help.

"Who knows whether you have come to the kingdom for such a time as this?" Mordecai asked (Esther 4:14).

After almost backing down and resisting the call to rise up, Esther bravely responded, "I'll do it. And if I die, so be it" (Esther 4:16, my paraphrase).

This was a huge moment not only in Esther's life but in the history of the Jewish people. So much was at stake. This young woman literally put her life on the line to save her nation—a shine-bright-in-the-dark moment if there ever was one. But I don't think this was the only time Esther shined. I like to think that Esther's life was full of those moments.

When she grieved the loss of her mother and father, she was born for that.

When she was chosen as a contestant in the beauty pageant for the role of queen, she was born for that.

When she became the favorite of the attendants and given special treatment, she was born for that.

When she won the pageant and became queen, she was born for that.

Each time Esther fought to flourish out of the spotlight, she moved closer to her moment in the spotlight. She may have been born to save the nation of Israel, but there were many steps in getting there, and she had to walk through that journey. And this makes me ask this question: What is so important about the spotlight?

Why do we put so much emphasis on what is seen by everyone? I think maybe the more important question is, whose spotlight are we most concerned about, God's or everyone else's? When we are happy to be in God's spotlight, it won't matter to us if we make it big anywhere else. Whether we have thirty followers on Instagram or thirty thousand, whether our song becomes a hit, or we get the main role, how we live our life in God's spotlight is most important. God creates us for a purpose and gives us the potential to let His light shine through us in any situation.

Esther could have chosen to remain neutral. Standing up for her people was inconvenient. Her husband, the king, didn't know she was Jewish, and to approach him without being invited was risking a death sentence. (I know, weird marriage, but that's how they rolled in those days.) Esther had to decide for herself how she would allow God to use her in this situation. He had given her this platform and this privilege for a purpose. Ultimately, Esther acted on it and saved the nation of Israel from being massacred.

I love how Esther's given name, Hadassah, means "myrtle," which is an evergreen shrub and herb. The myrtle makes a great houseplant and can be sheared or pruned frequently, which makes it a prime candidate for hedges. You could say the myrtle shrub could be used for protection, to act like a barrier or a gate. But it also blooms small, fragrant, white flowers and has a pleasant aroma when crushed. Esther proved her name when she gave her life to protect her people, and when a lovely fragrance was spread as a result of the difficulty she faced. But her Persian name, Esther, means "star." God loves to take an average, ordinary plant and give it the beautiful potential to shine bright like a star. It's what He does. It's who He is.

Glow in the Dark

On the worst day of my life, it felt as if parts of me broke apart. I felt as though I had been punched in the stomach, the jaw, the head, and the thighs, and that the disorienting pain and blurred vision from these blows would last forever. I was weaker than I'd ever been before.

In all of this, God's face was toward me. He saw me. His hand was on me. He was near, and I knew this not only because the Bible says that God is near to the brokenhearted (Psalm 34:18), but because I felt His nearness.

February 14, 2013
8 weeks, 56 days since Lenya died

What's in my heart today:
My heart is broken on this Valentine's Day. And I know God is near to the brokenhearted. So I know and believe God is near and I know and believe Lenya is with Him in His presence, so I even believe she's near because God is here. BUT because she's not her in body—she just seems so far. And my heart is aching. And Lord, You are the only One who can comfort me, so this morning I look to You and Your Word. Like Levi says, You are big enough to handle my fears and my doubts and my questions, so I come to You this morning. What I'm really struggling with is my parenting with Lenya. When it comes down to it, I was the harshest and the strictest with her. I was impatient and I feel like I didn't take care of her as I should've. I should've been at her five-year checkup with Levi. I should have made sure she had what she needed. I should have loved her better. I was learning

to parent her better. I was learning to speak her love language. I was learning how to teach her and how to handle her freak-out moments. I just want the chance to be even better. But I won't ever get the chance with her. Ever. I get the chance with Alivia, Daisy, and Clover. I'm struggling with Your love for me, Lord! I believe that Your love is perfect and unconditional, not based on what I do or don't do, but I think I'm having a hard time resting in that love. And not thinking I should've, could've, would've.

God had given Lenya to us, but she wasn't really ours to begin with. She belonged to Him. He just chose to give her to us on loan, to love and to teach, not to mention to learn from. And for a reason I won't fully understand until heaven, He chose to take her back. Not that God wanted it, but He allowed it.

When we look to the One who created us and breathed His breath in us, we shine. Psalm 34:5 says, "They looked to Him and were radiant, and their faces were not ashamed." We can shine in the darkness because we look to God—our Creator and our King, our Lord and our Father. If He is the sun, then we're the moon. We aren't the source of light; we get to reflect it. We flourish when we reflect Jesus.

Everything we do in the current season is preparing us for the next one. Levi and I call this *training for the trial we're not yet in.* Fighting to grow sets us up to glow in the dark, so each step is essential to the next. The flourishing life is all about being faithful with the small things and watching God handle the impossible.

It's interesting to me that plants don't only need sunlight to grow; they need darkness just as much. Some plants, like gardenias and chrysanthemums, actually need up to eighteen hours of darkness each day before they bloom. In the same way, humans need both light and darkness to flourish too.

Since Lenya went to heaven, I've experienced a piercing in my soul that has lurched me into feeling like I was so lost. I have felt like a tiny seed left in the dirt, in the crap, without any hope of feeling the warmth of the sun again. But when I can look at the dirt and the dark and see it not for what it feels like it is, but as the very ingredients that are shaping me into the person God has created me to be, that's when I experience warmth. That's where I see God is with me. That's where I cling to Him, no matter how I feel, and I see Him change my perspective, and see that I was born for this. I can shine in the middle of darkness, not because of who I am or what I do, but because of Whose I am and what He's done.

Jesus is the Light of the world, and because He is in me, I can shine so others can see Him. Jesus said, "You are the light of the world. A city that is set on a hill cannot be hidden. Nor do they light a lamp and put it under a basket, but on a lampstand, and it gives light to all who are in the house. Let your light so shine before men, that they may see your good works and glorify your Father in heaven" (Matthew 5:14–16).

Often, shining bright means letting God use our pain and heartache. If you've ever lit a glow stick, you know you have to crack it to induce the chemical reaction in the tube that makes it light up. If you want God to use you, know that it will most likely involve pain.

I know this statement has some tension to it. It's not easy to read or hear. God wants to use me? I'm totally up for that. It's most likely going to involve pain? Thank you, but no thank you and next, please. But isn't this exactly what Jesus said? "In this world you will have trouble" (John 16:33 NIV). That's not very encouraging or positive. It's pretty overbearing and harsh—and it's the truth.

But we don't stop with the trouble part. Jesus said next, "But be of good cheer, I have overcome the world." He doesn't say "Be of good cheer, your pain will end soon." Or "Be of good cheer, this ache will go away forever." Jesus was saying, "Cheer up! I'm here. I know exactly what's going on, and I have overcome this."

If we let God use what He has allowed to happen, He shines through us. When we stop pushing against or refusing to fight through the pain, we open up to His will and His way—a key step toward the flourishing life.

In the Fire, but Not Burned Up

Jewelers purposefully display diamonds on black velvet. The brilliance of these gems is magnified when they're laid against the dark backdrop. In the same way, beauty is unlocked when we're surrounded by darkness.

God gave a promise through an ancient prophet:

> "Fear not, for I have redeemed you;
> I have called you by your name;
> You are Mine.
> When you pass through the waters, I will be with you;
> And through the rivers, they shall not overflow you.
> When you walk through the fire, you shall not be burned."
> (Isaiah 43:1–2)

When we go through fire and allow God to use our pain, He won't let it burn us. We'll have scars, but He will heal the wounds. The scars will remind us of God's faithfulness and that He will use the pain for something brilliant.

In the third chapter of the book of Daniel, we read about three

When we go

through fire and

allow God to use

our pain, He won't

let it burn us.

young men who didn't just stand in the face of danger—they actually stood in the middle of it. Like, for real, inside a human-sized, wood-fired oven. These guys respectfully refused to bow down to the king, so he commanded that they be thrown inside this fiery furnace. The king was so out-of-control angry with these guys, he even told his armed guards to make the furnace seven times hotter than usual. It was such an inferno that the men who tossed the three guys in were killed just by being near it. It seems like the author really wanted us to feel the heat because the phrase "burning fiery furnace" is repeated eight times in the story.

What about the three guys in the fire? They didn't burn. Not only did they live to tell about it but not a single hair on their heads was singed. And to top it all off, they didn't even smell like smoke!

I believe it's possible for us to go through hell on earth and not be burned. The fire does not have to consume us, and it doesn't have to define us either. We don't have to smell like what we've lived through. Some of the most beautiful people I know (some of whose stories I will tell you more about later) have walked through great pain and simultaneously have held on to God with everything they have, with joy and with grace. We can pray what the psalmist prayed: "Every morning I lay out the pieces of my life on the altar and wait for your fire to fall upon my heart" (Psalm 5:3 TPT).

Embrace Your Superpower

Batman. Wonder Woman. Captain America. Spiderman. Black Widow. Besides fashioning epic spandex suits on their super-toned bodies, possessing a special superpower, and fighting for a greater purpose against evil, superheroes have another thing in common:

they have all endured a fight. They've had to overcome a tragedy, loss, or hardship that made them who they are.

Maybe this is why so many of us are drawn to superheroes. Seeing them struggle with adversity and become stronger as a result is comforting. Perhaps we're more like them than we think.

In *Captain Marvel*, Carol Danvers is a fighter pilot in the United States Air Force. Her mentor, Kree scientist Mar-Vell, is experimenting with a special light-speed engine. When the two attempt to test the engine in space, they are blasted out of the sky and forced to crash land. They try to escape, but their enemy, who shot them down, guns down Mar-Vell. In an attempt to keep her mentor's work from getting in the wrong hands, Carol destroys the engine, and it explodes in her face. But instead of destroying her, the engine infuses her with its power. The tragedy of the accident is what leads to Carol's superpower. Now every time she throws a punch, she has explosive power in her hands.

Like Carol Danvers, if we can absorb what we're going through, it then becomes possible to create space for God to do something powerful through it. Paul wrote, "For it is the God who commanded light to shine out of darkness, who has shone in our hearts to give the light of the knowledge of the glory of God in the face of Jesus Christ" (2 Corinthians 4:6). The same God who directed the light to shine in the midst of the darkness is the God who tells us to shine brightly—when life is good and when life hurts.

But the weight to shine is not on our shoulders. The weight to flourish is not for us to carry. The weight is on our Savior, the One we look to for grace, for hope, for life, for love. This is what gives me strength in my soul, boldness in my bones, and might in my mind. Because, really, I'm not that strong or self-disciplined or intentional or aware or selfless. I'm just so grateful that when I am weak, He is strong.

And just like a superhero, it's the difficulty we face that gives us strength. God can shine His glory like never before when we embrace the struggle. So go ahead—get out a cape and fancy spandex (with some added Spanx support as needed). No matter how dark your world has become, you were born to shine in it every step of the way, with His power in your fists.

3

Find Your Grit

I love my bed. I love the look and feel of it. The reclaimed wood frame topped with a Casper mattress. The bamboo pillows with sheets that are perfect for both the hot summer nights and the cold winter ones. The textured, bohemian bedspread handloomed in India. My bed is cozy, warm, inviting, welcoming. The best bed in the world. Believe me, I know. Because we travel so much, I sleep in countless hotel beds. The comfort factor of my bed wins every time.

But my adoration for my bed isn't just about the aesthetics and comfort or even the fact that I get to sleep with Levi; I just love being in my bed. Even on a good morning, when I'm excited for the day, I have a hard time launching myself out of it. When I finally emerge from my cocoon and start making the bed, I look forward to when I'll get to climb back in again.

My husband praises me for being so good about making the bed every morning, but it's mostly because doing this keeps me from getting back in it. Making the bed is important to me. I've heard it's an important part of being a Navy SEAL, too, so that kind of makes me feel like one of them—apart from the butt-kicking training and life-threatening situations, of course. The rest of the room can be in shambles, but if the bed is made, I know everything is going to be okay.

When Lenya left this earth, not even the best bed in the world could make me think everything was going to be okay. I remember waking up one morning, a week or so after she went to heaven. I lay in bed, staring at the ceiling. Sunlight softly filtered through the curtains. It was time to get up. But I couldn't; it would mean this nightmare wasn't a dream.

A wave of grief swelled upward and over me, a crushing weight. *This can't be true. Lenya can't be gone.*

Elsewhere in the house, life moved on as usual. It didn't stop because my heart was breaking all over again. Clover's diaper would have been ready to explode by then. I had to help Daisy get dressed. Alivia, who had just lost her best friend, would need a hug from me. My kids needed their mom.

As minutes slipped away, I wondered whether I would stay in bed if I didn't have little ones to care for. Probably. Who knew? I didn't care. I hurt. It felt right to stay there, to hide under the covers. *Jesus, help me. I can't do this on my own.*

A picture of Lenya from a year ago flashed in my mind. Her complexion was so clear and smooth to the touch.

When she was a month old, she contracted a respiratory virus, which led to severe allergies that caused painful rashes all over her body. She spent most of her early years itchy, fussy, and uncomfortable. When Lenya was nine months old, we had to drive 253 miles to the children's hospital in Spokane, Washington, to find out that she was failing to thrive and was undernourished. I felt like I failed at being a mom. Why couldn't I help her grow and develop as she was meant to? Why didn't I see the signs earlier and do something about it before it got worse?

More doctor visits. More tests. A one-day visit turned into a weeklong trip. We found out our little girl was allergic to dairy, soy, eggs, nuts, chicken, turkey, dogs, horses, grass, dust—basically everything in our home and in the state of Montana. I stopped breastfeeding Lenya right away and started her on a hypoallergenic formula. When she turned one and a half, she ate through a feeding tube, and she continued to see the specialist regularly until she was three, at which point we "threw the tubey in the trash," as we affectionately referred to that day.

Over time, we started to see small changes in Lenya's health. As she grew more comfortable and began to thrive, more of her personality emerged. Lenya was so sweet. She always made us laugh and loved to ask questions. She had a compassionate heart and was tender toward her sisters, though she also had a strong personality that challenged me when it came to disciplining her.

When Lenya was four, her nutritionist told us to introduce soy into her diet. Her body handled it like a champ. Same thing with wheat. The next thing on our list was peanuts. I remember Lenya lying in bed one night and telling me, "Mom, when I get to heaven, I'm gonna eat a whole box of peanut butter and a whole pack of cheese!"

"Yes, you will, sweetie. That will be so amazing!" I cheered, snuggling her close.

As a family, we talked about heaven all the time. For Lenya, talking about heaven was as natural as talking about Disneyland. She knew that to be in heaven meant to be with Jesus and to not deal with allergies or sadness. But when the transition from earth to heaven actually happened, it felt completely unnatural to me. It was too soon. It didn't make sense. I trusted God, but I hated it.

Blinking through tears brought on by my memories, I prayed for strength. With everything in me, I pushed off the covers and pulled myself out of bed. Tiptoeing down the stairs, careful not to wake the sleeping house, I couldn't help but wonder what Lenya was doing right then. I don't know exactly what people in heaven experience, but I pictured her sitting with Jesus, watching the sunrise, possibly eating peanut butter and cheese sandwiches.

It would have been easy to stay in bed that morning. The struggle of forcing myself to face the day would stay for a long time. But God planted in my soul a grit that helped me see that I could take the next step, the next breath, and the next challenge with His strength in my heart.

Don't Take It Easy

Rocky Balboa is a small-time boxer living in a rundown apartment. (Yes, he's a fictional character, but it kind of feels like he's real, right? There *is* a statue of him in Philly, after all.) He doesn't have anything to his name—just a passion for life and for boxing. He gets paid by a local bookie to beat up people for unpaid loans, but Rocky's got bigger dreams. While most people see him as a bum, this underdog chooses to go the distance. Take chances. Work harder. Believe in a future only he can see. Rocky has to fight in order to fight, shuffling between triumphs and failures.

Unlike Rocky, I frequently fall into trying to find the easiest route. I would be like a river and take the path of least resistance every time if I could. I would stay far away from difficulties and challenges and the hard things that will actually cause me to grow. I would stay in the cozy world of my bed.

Hiding in our hurt or pain is natural, comfortable, and familiar. It's harder to choose to walk toward what's painful. It seems so much

God planted in

my soul a grit that

helped me see

that I could take

the next step, the

next breath, and

the next challenge

with His strength

in my heart.

safer to stay put and not push forward. But if we can fight forward, in His strength, we let God heal us the way He wants to and cultivate in us a grit to keep going.

I love what Paul said in 1 Corinthians 9:26, "Thus I fight: not as one who beats the air." The Greek word for fight here is *pukteuo*, which means "to box." Another Greek word he used for fight is *agonizomai*, noted in 1 Timothy 6:12, which means "to contend perseveringly against opposition and temptation." These words are not flowery and dainty. They evoke gladiator-type images of battle and fight scenes from *Creed*. Not pretty. Not clean. Not polished. But messy, bloody, painful, and full of resolve, effort, energy, and stamina that's out of the ordinary. Wow, I'm exhausted just writing that.

This is our fight: To keep moving forward. To keep walking through the pain instead of numbing it. To keep taking the next step when you'd rather stop. To keep choosing to spend time with God, to pray and dive into His Word, to show up for church when you don't feel like going.

Even today, it takes everything in me to fight off the lethargy that can so easily overtake my body and soul. Since I started having babies about fourteen years ago, a good night's sleep has become a rare and precious jewel. Growing up, I could sleep through anything—thunderstorms, earthquakes (not joking!), and the midnight cries of younger siblings. Not so much anymore; I'm wide awake at the slightest cough or a dream-induced whimper. If I catch a few hours of uninterrupted sleep, it's a win. I'm coming to terms with this sleepless season, but I don't like it.

As I'm writing this, I'm in a cabin with my family and some dear friends. Everyone is sleeping, and I'm up so I can write. The sun is slowly beginning to rise over rolling foothills and rich green forest—shout-out to Montana living. But having had a late night absent of much-needed sleep and an early start to the morning, I'm struggling to keep my eyes open. I know I need to get good rest to have a healthy, strong soul. How can I function and be at my best when I'm so tired? Well, I drink some coffee, sneak in a nap when I'm able, and power through, as tired as I may feel. My friend Holly Furtick once said, "We have to choose to be a boss at the mornings." Sleep or no sleep, babies or no babies, energy or no energy; we can get up, make our beds, ask God for the strength we desperately need, and go.

As an Enneagram type nine, I have a tendency to be lazy, even slothlike. I gravitate toward the easy route, whatever demands the least energy or effort. Which means every day I fight against my nature in order to be sweet, to be kind, to grow spiritually, to develop my character, to honor my husband, and to be the mother I want my kids to remember had a smile on her face. When I don't feel like doing something, it generally makes it that much more important to do it.

We can't do only what's easy. If that were the case, most of us would quit our jobs, ditch our responsibilities, and lie on a beach all day. (Maybe that's just me?) And that also means we wouldn't have any relationships of great significance, our characters would lack depth, and we would not live the lives of purpose God has called us to.

A life that blooms with growth doesn't just happen. Progress requires effort and energy, stamina and sweat, persistence and perseverance.

I found out I was fast when I was in first grade and competed in the school Olympics (kind of a big deal, people!). I won the fifty-yard dash that year and learned that I liked to run fast. In eighth grade I decided to start training to be on the track team in high school, and my love-hate relationship with the sprint began. My first day, all I remember is running until I vomited, and then lying on my back watching the sky spin above me. I loved the sprint but hated the training. This first practice would launch me into the high school track team, where I competed in the 100-meter dash, the 200, the 4x100 relay, and the long jump.

When you're running to win, there's a fire under your feet. There's an intensity that acts as fuel to motivate action. Paul talked about this kind of fight in 1 Corinthians 9:24–25: "Do you not know that in a race all the runners run, but only one gets the prize? Run in such a way as to get the prize. Everyone who competes in the games goes into strict training. They do it to get a crown that will not last, but we do it to get a crown that will last forever" (NIV).

You might not be the biggest fan of exercise, but I want to encourage you to think of yourself as a *spiritual* athlete. You can put yourself through the kind of strict training Paul talked about. You can run a little harder. You can sprint, you can punch, you can give, you can love and serve others with a fervency in your soul. You are running your race. You are fighting to become the woman you were designed to be, and that will take daily effort.

I love SoulCycle. I have even been an instructor at a similar boutique spin studio in my town. I find the hardest part of spin class is toward the end, when I'm exhausted and sweaty, and my muscles burn because I've given everything I've got. The other day, I was at this point. My shoes were clipped in, but my legs had hit a wall. Sweat dripped into my eyes, and my calves and quads raged in defiance, telling me they couldn't go any longer. I was about to tell myself to slow down and back off the effort when the instructor yelled out, "Don't stop because you're tired. Push harder. Push through this because this could bring the breakthrough you've been wanting!"

I needed to hear this. I needed to ride hard if I was going to do anything of real significance in my body. If things get hard, it doesn't mean we back down; it means we push through. And we don't push through just to get it over with; we push through with an added effort to get the most out of the challenge.

Sounds great, right? But how do we actually do this in life? We can start by doing what we don't feel like doing.

Just Do It (Especially When You Don't Want To)

A week before Lenya went to heaven, Levi led a funeral for a teenage girl who had died of cancer. He talked to and prayed with her mother, but afterward we didn't see her for about five years, until we ran into her at church. After the service, she told us that her daughter's death created in her a pain so deep she started abusing substances. She finally got the help she needed, and at the time we reconnected, she was seven months sober. She was just beginning the journey through grief, because she hadn't initially dealt with the pain. She thought she could mask it or hide from it, but what she needed was to deal with it straight on. We can try to walk around the pain or avoid it altogether, but it's going to find a way to come out.

So often, we want to escape when things get tough. But that's not what's going to help us. Running away from the difficulty will keep us from the growth we were meant to experience. Fighting means the most when you feel like doing it the least. Fighting forward means advancing in the face of danger when everything in you tells you to retreat. In the words of my favorite Peloton instructor, Ally Love, during one of her rides, "If it's not a challenge, then I don't want it."

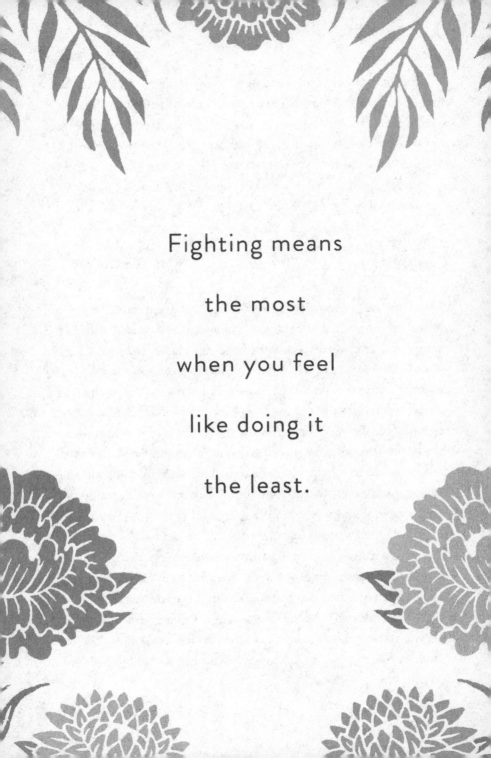

Fighting means

the most

when you feel

like doing it

the least.

Levi calls this "running toward the roar," which he wrote about in his book *Through the Eyes of a Lion*.

When you run from things that scare you, you move toward danger, not away from it. If you fail to face your fears, they will always be right there behind you. You must suppress the little voice inside that's telling you to get out of Dodge. It is not your friend. When you feel that panicky fight-or-flight sensation and you want to run away, do the opposite. Run toward the roar.

When Lenya went to heaven, we made a conscious choice to run toward the roar. We did the things we didn't want to do; particularly, that meant feeling every ounce of grief. We wouldn't turn away the tears. We wouldn't stash away the pain for another day. We wouldn't avoid places or people that reminded us of our little girl waiting in heaven. We would fight through the grief. We would fight to stick together. We would fight as God worked to heal our beat-up hearts, whatever that looked like and however long it would take.

A few weeks after Lenya died, we received a package from the hospital. Levi and I knew what it was. We could have just tossed it in the trash or put it away unopened in the closet, but we didn't. We sat down, braced ourselves for impact, and asked God to help us do this really hard thing.

Let me pause here to clarify that sometimes it's impossible to know exactly the right thing to do. We had many regrets in those early days, including deciding not to have a viewing. People we trusted said we needed to do what we felt was right, but we regret not letting Alivia and those closest to us say goodbye to Lenya that way.

It's important to walk toward what's scary. If we don't want to do something, that usually indicates the very road we should take.

So we decided to walk the road of opening up the package from the hospital, and, therefore, opening up our grief.

In the package were the clothes Lenya wore the night she went to heaven. Her Fresh Life red pajama pants (as she liked to call them). Clover's baby socks, because Lenya loved squeezing into her little sister's clothes. Underwear smelling of urine. Having been cut off her body, most of her clothing was torn. Levi and I wept and wept. We said out loud how much we loved Lenya and how much we missed her and how much we hated that she was not with us for the rest of our lives on earth.

I wrote in my journal later that night:

This is so stupid hard. I hate this! I miss Lenya. I want her. But soon and very soon I will see her. We will hug and run and dance and sing. Angels brought her to heaven.

I needed the reminder that the tragedy that left a gaping hole in our world was still the moment when angels led her into the presence of Jesus.

I wasn't quick to throw out the last pajamas Lenya wore. I held them for a bit, almost as an offering to God, surrendering my heartache—something I would have to fight to do over and over and over again.

So often when we endure pain, we want to run from the very One who designed us, knows us, and has a plan for our lives. But God wants us to run to Him. He loves us and He knows what we need to know: that our source of healing and power and strength comes only from Him. Whatever your struggle, don't run away from Him; run *toward* Him. He is big enough and strong enough and loves you enough to handle it and to heal you. He is the only answer to the ache within your soul and your struggle.

We have to fight to choose to do the hard things. But here's good news for us: Jesus gave us an example to follow. Throughout the Gospels, He showed us what was most important. Many times He would be on His way somewhere but would take a moment with someone. Jesus showed us that regardless of the schedule, what took precedence was doing what God led Him to do and going where God called Him to go. As we follow Jesus, we follow His example. We do the hard things. We have late nights. We have early mornings. We have uncomfortable conversations. We fast and we pray. We choose kindness when we want to be rough. We pour our hearts and souls into all we do because that's what God has called us to. What we put into our lives is what we'll get out of it. It's worth it because God has plans *for* us, but He also has plans for others *through* us.

Butterfly Zombies

God designed you to live to your full potential. When you choose not to dig a little deeper and fight to get the most out of your life, well, it reminds me of a very sad story.

A friend of Clover's gave her a fun, out-of-the-box present for her seventh birthday. Never mind that our daughter's birthday is in January and we finally had her party in April. Part of the delay was because of poor planning on my part, but also because we travel quite a bit as a family. (Hey, the struggle is real. Let's never speak of this again.) Anyway, the gift was a create-your-own butterfly garden complete with living caterpillars. What a sweet idea, right?

Well, around the same time as Clover's belated birthday party, I was also planning for our family vacation scheduled soon after. In the midst of the celebration and the vacation prep, the box of live caterpillars somehow ended up at the bottom of some other boxes of toys and stayed there—oh man, I hate even admitting this—for four weeks.

Warning: if you have a weak stomach, you may not want to read what happened next.

Clover opened up the box, and the caterpillars that were meant to be housed in a large, airy mesh habitat were all still in their little containers. Maybe two of them, at best, looked healthy. Some were dead. The rest were ghostly, sickly versions of themselves. These caterpillars were created to grow a chrysalis around themselves, in which they would transform into butterflies and then use their muscles to fight their way out of the cocoon. Ultimately, these transformed creatures were designed to fly and flutter and drink sweet things and be fruitful and create more butterflies. But what I saw were zombie butterflies. They were nearly dead.

It breaks my heart that I totally failed these beautiful creatures. Having grown up in Monterey, California, where the monarch butterflies migrate, I should have known better and been more careful.

What I'm trying to help you see is that God intends for you to become the most fruitful, most vibrant, and most-like-Jesus version of you that you were born to be. If you can lean in, embrace the challenge, and fight through the hard things, you will start to see the joy in the heartache. You will even start getting out of bed in the morning with a greater sense of purpose, no matter how much you love your bed.

God is strengthening and using you more than it may seem. Keep going. You're stronger than you think you are. Keep walking in His great love for you. Keep doing the hard things. Because in the words of one of my spin instructors, "Easy doesn't make you stronger."

4

Keep Your Guard Up

Pain is such an unlikely strengthener. You would think the presence of pain would make us weaker because of how debilitating it is—whether we've been hurt in our relationships or we're dealing with trauma from the past or we're struggling with anxiety, depression, or insecurity. Pain seems to rob us of our strength and can leave us feeling stuck in a pit wondering if we'll ever be rescued. It's tempting to allow pain to steal from us the abundant life Jesus came to give us. But if we want to grow stronger, we're going to need to look at our pain differently.

One of my favorite people in the Bible is Joseph. There's so much to learn from him, like his vision for his life, his work ethic, his fight, resolve, and perspective. Joseph didn't have an easy life. His own brothers left him for dead in a pit. He was sold into slavery, falsely accused of rape, and thrown into prison. Most of his youth seemed to be wasted because he spent at least twelve years behind bars for a crime he didn't commit.

Joseph endured the kind of circumstances that would cause anyone to become bitter, resentful, and hardened. He could have had a "that's the story of my life" mentality. He could have thrown in the towel, blamed someone else for his issues, and quit. But he didn't.

When Joseph was suddenly released from prison and, in a miraculous act, promoted as second-in-command over the nation of Egypt, he received a surprise visit. His brothers stood before him, the very ones who set in motion his tragic life. But here's the twist: Joseph didn't seek revenge. He didn't return the favor and throw his brothers into a pit. In a powerful act of reconciliation, he forgave them. "You meant evil against me," he said to his brothers, "but God meant it for good, in order to bring it about as it is this day, to save many people alive" (Genesis 50:20).

"You meant evil against me; but God meant it for good." Those eleven words could change your life. Joseph realized that even in a pit, even chained as a slave, even stuck behind bars, if he continued to love and serve God, he could push through the pain and come out stronger on the other side.

Only You Can Keep Your Own Guard Up

I like how pastor Brian Houston says that our spirit is our responsibility. Similarly, my husband also says that the most important person you lead is yourself. No one else can choose Jesus for you. No one else can make the right decision for you. No one else can push you harder.

Joseph couldn't choose what happened in his life, but it was Joseph, not anyone else, who made the decisions on *how* he would live. He chose to help two men in prison who couldn't help him and ended up forgetting about him. He decided to work hard and live an honorable life. He chose to run away from his boss's sexy wife who was throwing herself at him. He decided to forgive his brothers. No one else did these things for him. Joseph made the decision to live right, and he did it. This kind of living takes commitment and true grit. It also requires constant training.

I told you earlier that I also love boxing. One of the most important rules in boxing is to keep your guard up. I read advice from a trainer that claimed everything begins and ends with the on-guard position. Why keep your guard up in a fight? Easy—you'll get hit more if you don't.

Recently, we watched all the Rocky movies with our kids. Whenever he would drop his hands and allow himself to get hit, I found myself yelling at the screen, "Put your hands up, Rocky! Guard yourself! What are you thinking?!"

Another essential part of boxing is focus. You shouldn't look anywhere other than where your opponent is. Get distracted even for a second, and you're going to get hit. You have to be on guard. And only you can be on your own guard.

When it comes to guarding our souls, one of the strongest tactics is Scripture. I love memorizing Bible verses with my children. Their little voices reciting God's Word is one of my favorite sounds. One of the most special videos we have of Lenya is of her saying Psalm 23 when she was three. It's a precious and powerful thing when children hide God's Word in their hearts and declare it out loud.

Recently, I was memorizing Ephesians 6:11–18 with some of the women on our church's staff. I also started to teach it to my kids.

Put on the full armor of God, so that you can take your stand against the devil's schemes. For our struggle is not against flesh and blood, but against the rulers, against the authorities, against the powers of this dark world and against the spiritual forces of evil in the heavenly realms. Therefore put on the full armor of God, so that when the day of evil comes, you may be able to stand your ground, and after you have done everything, to stand. Stand firm then, with the belt of truth buckled around your waist, with the breastplate of righteousness in place, and with your feet fitted with the readiness that comes from the gospel of peace. In addition to all this, take up the shield of faith, with which you can extinguish all the flaming arrows of the evil one. Take the helmet of salvation and the sword of the Spirit, which is the word of God. And pray in the Spirit on all occasions with all kinds of prayers and requests. With this in mind, be alert and always keep on praying for all the Lord's people. (NIV)

I see the word *stand* four times in this scripture. Paul was telling the church to stand in the struggle, to stand in the battle, and to stand firm—but not in their own strength. This is important to understand as we fight to flourish: admitting that we're weak on our own and need the power of God to engage in battle changes how we live.

Earlier in Ephesians 6, Paul offered markers for how believers can flourish in their roles as children, fathers, employees, and employers. He ended these instructions with verse 10: "Finally, be strong in the Lord and in His mighty power" (NIV). Boom. The key is right here: be strong *in the Lord*, in His mighty power.

Keep your guard up. Make His strength your strength, and you'll be able to be the best fighter you can be.

Ruth Bell Graham was a boss. I have been forever changed by her life. I love reading about her, about how she loved and supported her family and her husband, Billy. When she died at the age of eighty-seven, her namesake daughter, Ruth, said this about

Admitting that

we're weak on

our own and need

the power of

God to engage

in battle changes

how we live.

her mom: "Her happiness and fulfillment did not depend on her circumstances. She was a lovely, beautiful and wise woman because early in life she made Christ her home, her purpose, her center, her confidant and her vision." Her husband, Billy, said, "She was a spiritual giant, whose unparalleled knowledge of the Bible and commitment to prayer were a challenge and inspiration to everyone who knew her. My favorite photograph shows her sitting on our front porch at sunrise, quietly reading her Bible and sipping coffee—her daily routine for many years."

#Goals. Rising early, drinking coffee, and reading the Bible. This simple discipline shaped her life. It was her way of keeping her guard up. And it can be yours too.

Enjoy the One Who Loves You the Most

Our youngest daughter, Clover Dawn, now seven, was by far our wiggliest, on-the-move baby (that is, until our son, Lennox, came along). Our other three daughters are similarly wild and free, but as far as the baby stage goes, Clover stands out. From when she was about six months old, whenever I would hold her, she'd squirm around in my arms, twisting her whole body to see what else might be going on or what her sisters might be up to. Even now, she's always on the move, quick to jump into the next, more exciting thing.

I remember one time I picked Clover up and she immediately tried to wiggle her way out of my arms. Playfully frustrated, I looked at her and said, "Clover! Just enjoy me!"

I immediately thought that's probably what God says to me so often. "Jennie, just enjoy Me! Don't get distracted by others or by what you think you need to do instead. Enjoy Me."

There are times I don't receive what I need from my relationship with God because I'm not enjoying Him as I was meant to. I get distracted way too easily. I pray or try to pray, but all I can think about is everything else that I don't need to be thinking about in that moment. It never fails: I sit down with my coffee, tea, hot water, or green juice (I change it up all the time because I weirdly need variety and change in my life). I get ready to engage in time alone with God, but my mind gets bombarded by my to-do list. Things I never think about or remember conveniently make their sassy little way to the front of my brain. The people I forgot to text back. The laundry that's so savagely attacking my hallway. The organizing that needs to be done in every single room of the house. It's a serious fight to focus. Every day.

I wonder if Jesus had a similar struggle. Perhaps that's why the Bible mentions several times how He would go to a solitary place to pray. This seems intentional. Maybe we need to find a special spot where we can power off our minds and tune in to Him. I like to position myself where I can't see the dishes or the looming pile of laundry or our schedule. I know they're there, but if I can't see them and instead see clean and uncluttered countertops, I help myself focus a little better.

The One Thing That's Needed

Distraction can be our biggest adversary. We see this perfectly illustrated when two sisters, Martha and Mary, invited Jesus over to their house. Mary, a good host, spent her time talking with Jesus. Martha, also a good host, checked off her to-do list, which was the length of her dining room table. With a hustle in her step, she was in the kitchen trying to set the table, flavor the sauce, and wipe down the counters. Feeling overwhelmed, Martha poked her head into the living room and with a dramatic sigh said, "Jesus, don't You care that my sister isn't helping me? Tell her to help me!" (Luke 10:40, my paraphrase).

Jesus replied with such tenderness. "Martha, Martha, you are worried and troubled about many things. But one thing is needed, and Mary has chosen that good part, which will not be taken away from her" (vv. 41–42).

Mary might have known what was most important. But I think more than that, she just genuinely loved Jesus and loved hearing Him speak. Mary chose to sit at His feet. She made Jesus the front and center of her life. She said yes to the best thing, the one thing that couldn't ever be taken away—time spent with her Savior. If we focus on what can't be taken away, then even when who or what we love is taken away from us, our relationship with Jesus stands strong.

I hate to admit it, but I so relate to Martha. I've spent my fair and unfortunate share of time whining, getting distracted, and obsessing over my to-do list. Looking back, I feel ashamed at the times I chose to *do* instead of *be*.

I love Jesus' response to Martha. He didn't blame or shame her. Instead, He corrected her with gentleness. There was nothing wrong with Martha wanting to make this lunch epic. Someone's gotta be the party planner! The problem was that she put the emphasis on the preparations and not on the Person she was preparing for. It can be easy, especially in church, to forget the reason we serve because we're so focused on *what* we need to do instead of *why* we need to do it—bringing it back to the simplicity of loving God and others.

I think sometimes Mary gets a bad rap as being unhelpful or lazy because Martha was the one doing all the work. Maybe Mary had already done her part. Maybe she had gone to the grocery store in the morning or had taken care of the meal prep the night before. Or maybe she really hadn't helped, and that's why Martha was so bugged. I don't know. The point is, Mary made Jesus the priority.

A seasoned woman I know once taught me that it's not even really about positioning Jesus *above* my to-do list. It's about making Him *the center* of it. Like this:

Jesus is the center, and everything flows from our relationship with Him. As much of a fight as it feels to live that way, it's essential. When we make our relationship with Jesus our priority, we lay the foundation for our future.

Developing that relationship is not about perfection. If you're trying to find the formula for getting it right all the time, good luck with that and let me know how it goes! Not to be rude or negative, but we won't be perfect, ever—and that's not the goal. The goal is growing more in love with Jesus and becoming more like Him. We become like the people we spend time with. Spend time with Jesus, and you'll know Him more, love what He loves, do what He does, hate what He hates, speak what He speaks. This sets the pace for our lives, and that can't be taken away.

Treasure It Up

We have more access to the Bible in a variety of translations than ever before. It's so important for our spiritual health that we do more than just rush through our reading plans, quickly find something to post on social media, and get on with our days. I'm only saying that because I've done it! Time spent in the Word and in prayer is never wasted time. It's a guardrail we set around our lives. It protects us, strengthens us, refreshes us—and it activates growth. We may not feel the immediate effects, but over time, engaging with God produces a deep work.

We planted apple trees a few years ago. The gardeners who helped us pick the right ones told us not to worry if the apples grow differently each year, because what happens one year is essential and helpful for the growth that happens the next. They were right. The first year, the apples were tiny and bitter and horrible. We picked them and immediately threw them away. The following year, the apples were bigger, and there were more of them, but they still tasted sour. The third year, we had double the apples, and some weren't that bad. We actually made an apple pie with them (and if my baking skills were a little stronger, maybe I would have made pies for the neighbors). This year, they were the same as the previous year—not amazing, but also not bad.

Our apple trees are undergoing a deep transformation. The watering, the sunlight, and the care of the soil is doing much more

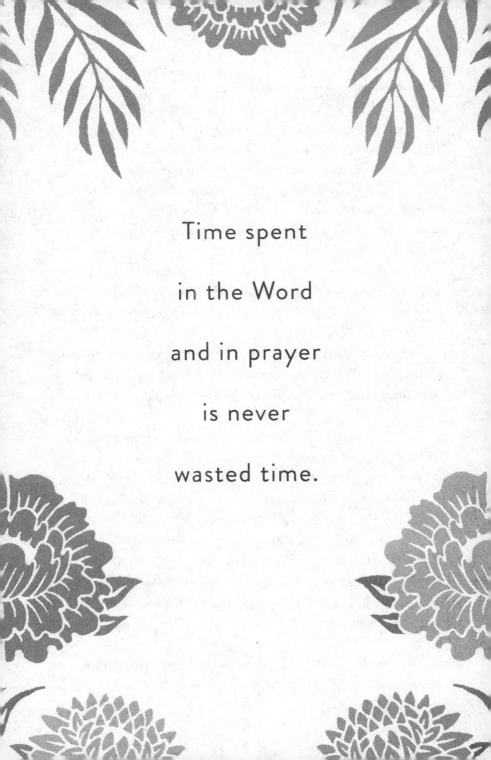

Time spent

in the Word

and in prayer

is never

wasted time.

than growing apples; it's actually growing a more robust tree that will be strong enough to create delicious and better fruit. I'm excited to see what we're going to get next year. Just as caring for the trees produces tasty fruit over time, when you invest in your time with God, growth, transformation, and fruit are inevitable.

Psalm 119 tells us what this dependence on God's Word looks like in our hearts: "How can a young person stay pure? By obeying your word. . . . I have hidden your word in my heart, that I might not sin against you" (vv. 9, 11 NLT).

I have hidden your word in my heart. The Hebrew word for hide is *tsaphan*, translated "treasure up." We gather up God's Word. We treasure it. We study it. We memorize it. We meditate on it. We soak in its truth.

Jesus compared receiving the Word of God to a seed being planted. In Mark 4:3–8, He made this analogy through a story, something He often did to help people relate truth to their own lives.

"Listen! Behold, a sower went out to sow. And it happened, as he sowed, that some seed fell by the wayside; and the birds of the air came and devoured it. Some fell on stony ground, where it did not have much earth; and immediately it sprang up because it had no depth of earth. But when the sun was up it was scorched, and because it had no root it withered away. And some seed fell among thorns; and the thorns grew up and choked it, and it yielded no crop. But other seed fell on good ground and yielded a crop that sprang up, increased and produced: some thirtyfold, some sixty, and some a hundred."

The key to sowing is good ground—a ready heart. When we receive God's Word as we read, study, or hear it preached at church, we welcome it deep down in our souls. We cultivate a love and anticipation for Him to speak to us through it. This is how we truly treasure up God's Word in our hearts. We consider it a treasure, and we act like it is.

Hiding something requires a mind-set of knowing the need for something later. We stash it away so no one else can find it and so that we can save it for later. Regardless of what your intake of Scripture looks like now, see the time you spend in God's Word as storing up or hiding, a little here, a little there. And as you treasure it up, you're setting yourself up to be stronger, and your future self will thank you.

SOAP Style

So we understand that diving into Scripture on a regular basis is important. But how do we do it? How do we approach a divinely inspired book written thousands of years ago by various authors in a foreign language and in so many different translations? I'm getting stressed out just writing that. Is it as simple as just reading it? Well, yes-ish.

A good place to start is to pray and ask God for help. He wants to speak to us, but we need Him to open our spiritual eyes so that we can understand what we're reading and see how it applies to us specifically. Then, open up the Bible and start reading. When we read together as a family, we always pray out loud first, "Dear God, open our eyes to see glorious truths in Your Word."

I recently shared with Alivia a simple method that has helped me: SOAP. It's not something I made up. It's a real thing, and I promise it's not complicated. All it takes is a Bible, a journal, and a few minutes to yourself.

- **S—Scripture**: Just start reading. The Gospels are an amazing place to begin. Write out the verses that stand out to you.
- **O—Observe**: Reflect on what you read. Ask questions. What word or phrase jumps out at you in the passage? What was taking place? Who was there? Did anything unusual or different happen? Feel free to dig a little deeper and use resources like the Logos Bible app or the Blue Letter Bible, which can help you discover the meaning of words in the original language and the background of the passage. Write down your observations.
- **A—Apply**: Here's where you get to connect what you've read with your life right now. Is there something you need to change or start doing? Put on your gardening or boxing gloves and write down how you can apply these truths to the season you're in.
- **P—Prayer**: Talk with God. He's spoken to you through His Word, and now you get to thank Him and ask Him to help you act on what you've learned. Write out your prayer.

If you have children, set the goal for studying and memorizing Scripture together. God tells us,

"Commit yourselves wholeheartedly to these words of mine. Tie them to your hands and wear them on your forehead as reminders. Teach them to your children. Talk about them when you are at home and when you are on the road, when you are going to bed and when you are getting up. Write them on the doorposts of your house and on your gates, so that as long as the sky remains above the earth, you and your children may flourish in the land the LORD swore to give your ancestors." (Deuteronomy 11:18–21 NLT)

Commit. Tie. Wear. Teach. Talk. Write. This sounds a lot like school to me, and I think that's the point. Whether you have made the decision to homeschool or are a public-school family, whether you're living the school-hacking life or do private school, we are all called to teach our kids God's Word. It can be a struggle a lot of the time, and it's so much easier to not do it. My husband and I have found that once we say, "Let's read the Bible, kids!" one or two of them will run away, one will start whining, and another will suddenly disappear to the bathroom. If you can relate, don't quit. Keep fighting for that time. And remember you can do this anywhere—at home, or like Moses said, on the road. Use every opportunity to talk to your children about God's faithfulness, goodness, and provision. Make it a part of everyday life, because it is.

Reading the Bible with my kids has created some of the most special moments in my life. But even if you don't have kids, consider reading a kids' Bible anyway. It's helpful to read the Bible in a way a child can comprehend.

Before Lenya went to heaven, we were reading through the story of Esther in a children's Bible. I can't even tell you which one it was because the cover is torn off. Lenya loved this particular story so much that she had memorized it. I remember the line she and Alivia would always recite together (or, let's be honest, fight for who would say it first): "Esther twirled her dress in a perfect circle and smiled at the king." I thought of this when Lenya went to be with Jesus. I imagined her twirling her dress in a perfect circle and smiling at her King.

Don't underestimate the long-term impact of your daily intake of Scripture. Let it set the pace for your life. Storing up the Word of God in your heart will unleash a new perspective on where you are. You will gain strength in areas of weakness. You will find healing even in the darkest of places.

Anytime I let myself get distracted or I cut short my time with God because I've got too many things fighting for my attention, I have to remind myself to get my guard back up. Focus. Hands up. Elbows in, leaning into what God's saying to me. I have to be persistent in just being still and enjoying Him. Whether I'm hurting or happy, I want to be ready, listening for God's instruction, committed to not backing down.

5

Get Back in the Ring

Lenya's body lies in a grave on top of a hill. On a clear day, the Montana sky stretches wide and blue, and you can see Glacier National Park in the distance. It's breathtaking. But on this particular day, it was hard to see, let alone look for, the beauty.

I drove by myself past the cemetery. Sobbing, I felt myself spiraling. "I don't know if I can handle not having Lenya here with me," I cried. The ache in my chest tightened into a knot that would seemingly never be soft again. Unfamiliar and destructive thoughts began to bombard my mind.

You're not strong enough.
It's not worth the pain.
You're not going to make it.
Just give up.

This kind of self-talk was foreign to me. Without a doubt, these thoughts were suicidal in nature. Where did they even come from? There I was, a leader, a pastor's wife, a mom in my thirties. I'd never before even entertained the idea of giving up. Yet the thoughts kept coming. Probably the worst was the whisper trying to convince me that if I just accidentally ran my car off the road, I'd be much better off, my family would be okay, and best of all, I'd be with Lenya.

Looking back through a rational lens, giving up didn't make any sense. Yes, it was horrible that my daughter had been taken from me, but the reality was I had three more sweethearts to be a mom to. I also had a husband and a marriage worth fighting for. My family needed me. My church needed me. My community needed me. This was not the time to panic and throw in the towel. This was the moment to wipe the sweat off my forehead, seal up the cut on my eyebrow, slip in a mouthguard, and get back in the ring. No matter how tired I was. No matter how beat up I felt.

In that moment, I responded the only way I knew how: I brought God into the situation. I recited out loud Bible verses that gave me strength, such as "He who is in [me] is greater than he who is in the world" (1 John 4:4). And I echoed self-affirming, Scripture-based truths, such as "I am called to this. I may feel hopeless. I may feel like there is no way I'm going to make it through this. I feel like I might actually be physically crushed by this, but God is with me. I've trained for this. I'm stronger than I think I am. I'm adored by my husband and my kids more than I think I am. I was born for this." When I'm in a situation I don't understand, I speak the words I do know.

One More Round

Giving up when life becomes overwhelming is tempting. For many people, it feels like their only option. We know the celebrities who made headlines for taking their own lives, and some of us have felt this pain personally because of loved ones who chose this heart-breaking route. The suicide rate is alarming, and it keeps growing.

There is a way through the pain, the loss, the heartache. There is hope, whether you feel it or not. There is strength to take the next breath, the next step. God is near. He loves you, and He is with you in your pain. Please don't go through this struggle alone—you weren't meant to. You might think there is no one there for you, but there is. Call someone you trust and who loves you. Bring that person in, no matter how you think they'll react. But most of all, know that there's a way through this because of Jesus. He makes a way where there is no way. He is the answer to our darkest pain and our deepest need. Just wait; there's more for you—more for your future, for your family. Dawn is coming.

Lean in close for a second, and listen to this: you are the only you. There is no one like you. No one else has your DNA. Your finger-prints are unique to you. You may look like someone or remind others of somebody else, but that person isn't you. No one can do what you do. No one else can fill the space God gave you to fill. You are called to be who you are, the best version of you. Let this sink into your spirit, and let it give you the push you need to get back in the ring if you have tapped out of this round.

I love what Rocky Balboa tells his son in *Rocky IV*: "If you go one more round when you don't think you can, that makes all the difference in your life." Don't think of the whole fight; that can get overwhelming for anyone. Think of the round you're in right now. And if that is still too much, then focus on this hit, this punch, this step.

When I get overwhelmed, it helps me to take a step back, get some perspective, see this fight for what it is, and then get back in the ring. When you don't give up, God shows up. He gives you what you need—Himself—for this round, and the next, and the one after that.

When you

don't give

up, God

shows up.

When dark thoughts come, when you feel like giving up, make a conscious choice to counter those lies with what God says, with His truth. Give yourself the opportunity to stay in the fight.

You are the only one who can make the choice that you're going to fight to flourish. No one else can choose it for you. And the good news is you will win this match, because Jesus has already won the war. All you have to do is fight today. One day at a time. One round at a time. One punch at a time.

Know Your Enemy Because He's Real

How many times do you feel yourself surrounded by inner dialogue or thoughts that are negative and that drain the life out of you? If you're anything like me, probably more times than you'd care to admit. Dark thoughts love to plague my mind in the midnight hour, when I'm exhausted but can't sleep.

Let me give you a peek into this world. I wrote in my journal while we were on a tour of the country preaching around the topic of my husband's book *I Declare War*:

February 8, 2019

It's been a rough few weeks. Having these horrible thoughts. Wishing God would just take me away, so Levi could move on and marry someone better because he deserves that. That's my fight. . . . And I'm honestly really tired of it. I feel so alone. The enemy wants me to stay there. He wants me to feel like I'm alone in this and if anyone found out they'd think I'm crazy. But I really feel like I am.

I know. It's pretty dark. And I'm not entirely sure if I should have even shared one of my deepest and most painful journal entries. Too late now. I bring you into my struggles to remind you that you are not alone and that there's a way through.

I mention that we were on tour preaching a message all about fighting the battle within, because that is the truth of doing what God's called you to do. When you step out in faith to follow Him and attempt to share the truth with others, you can get bombarded with lies like these:

You're too old for this.
You're too young for this.
You're not smart enough.
You're not the one for the job.
Someone else can do it better.
Nobody cares about you.
You're all alone.
No one else struggles with this.

The one whispering these things to you is the Devil, who is our enemy. He's real and he wants nothing more than to steal, kill, and destroy. The Bible says that the Devil roams around like a roaring lion seeking whom he may devour (1 Peter 5:8). *Devour*—well, that's not a very gentle word. Or delicate. Or nice. This enemy of our souls wants to take us out and keep us down.

The Contemporary English Version says that the Devil is "sneaking around to find someone to attack." The Enemy is studying our every move, what we do and what we don't do. He is taking notes of our weaknesses, our bad habits, what tempts us, and what brings us over the edge, and he will use all these things against us. He will do anything to pull a Karate Kid move, fight dirty, and sweep our legs out from under us. He doesn't want to just punch us in the mouth or break our nose; he wants a TKO, a total and technical knockout.

The Devil wants to kill us, sabotage our callings, destroy our relationships, spoil our present, and dismantle our future. He wants to annihilate us before we can ever start to flourish. I know this is pretty intense. I'm not trying to scare you away; I just need you to be aware of whom you're dealing with. If you don't know you're in a fight and that you have an enemy, you'll stumble around without traction or forward progress in your journey.

The truth is that the Enemy can't take us out of God's hand. But if we let him, he can make us unusable for the kingdom through his attempts to distract us, dilute our influence, or make us feel insecure and unworthy. If he is successful, he will keep us from having an impact in this world.

I recently took a self-defense class with some friends. It was life altering. (I highly recommend you take a course near you. It will change the way you see yourself and your surroundings.) The instructor told us about a study in which convicted criminals were shown a video of random people walking down a busy city street. They were then asked to point out which of these people they would hypothetically target. A pattern quickly emerged. These perpetrators chose their victims based on nonverbal signals, including body language, posture, and awareness. These were markers of strengths or weaknesses. For example, a woman who slowly shuffled along, her eyes peeled to the ground, would be seen as an easy target. One who walked with confidence, aware of her surroundings, would not be.

This is what the Enemy does. He's on the prowl looking for the weak. The lost. The underconfident. And he's looking to take them out.

Let's pause for a sec. Some of you might be thinking, *But, Jennie,*

I am weak! I get it. I am too! But that's actually a good thing, because the Bible says, "Let the weak say, 'I am a warrior'" (Joel 3:10 ESV). It also says that God's grace is sufficient for us because His power is made perfect in weakness. This means we can brag about our weakness so that the power of Jesus can work in us and make us strong (2 Corinthians 12:9). While your flesh may be weak, the spirit of the living God in you makes you strong. The reason we can be weak and declare that we are warriors is because of Christ. We are confident because His picture is on our seed packet. This is what faith in action looks like.

God has shown me that even in my darkest season of grief, I can find joy. I just have to fight to embrace it.

Even Though, I Will

On February 25, 2013, sixty-seven days after Lenya went to heaven, I got up early and spent a luxurious block of time with Jesus before everyone else got up. I read the Bible, prayed, learned, and wept. I also thumbed through my journal entries from the previous two months. I found so much sorrow and heartache.

> There's just a hole, a void, but the scary thing is that it's normalizing and I hate it. I don't want this to become normal. I don't want to be apart from Lenya any longer! But I know this is a light affliction. It doesn't feel like it though. Oh Lord, God. Fill this emptiness with You. Draw me in. Closer! Closer! I need You so desperately.

> Watched some Lenya TV, the video of her dance recital. The words of the song went "When I grow up in a year or two or

three . . ." I started bawling. Aching. Missing. It's morning now, missing my little early bird.

In Seattle, I've been having a hard day as images of Lenya when she died keep coming to my mind. It was so traumatic. So terrible. But she took her last breath in Levi's arms and took her first breath in heaven. I have to keep remembering that her suffering wasn't prolonged, it was quick. But I hate it! I hate it so much! But I also have to keep reminding myself that Jesus defeated death and the grave and has shone light in the darkness.

While grace and trust and truth weaved in and around the grief, on this morning, God was showing me to fully live this day, to find joy in this moment.

Psalm 16:11 tells us that in God's presence is fullness of joy. I think of how important it's been for me to choose to have a joyful heart, even in the midst of situations I can't control. When joy surrounds our hearts, it doesn't matter what else is surrounding it. It makes us impervious to what we're going through. The prophet Habakkuk gave us a brilliant picture of this mind-set:

> Even though the fig trees have no blossoms,
>> and there are no grapes on the vines;
> even though the olive crop fails,
>> and the fields lie empty and barren;
> even though the flocks die in the fields,
>> and the cattle barns are empty,
> yet I will rejoice in the LORD!
>> I will be joyful in the God of my salvation!
> The Sovereign LORD is my strength!

> He makes me as surefooted as a deer,
> able to tread upon the heights. (3:17–19 NLT)

A little background is helpful. Habakkuk was a frustrated prophet. In this book he was describing the nation of Judah at a low point in history. Everything was going wrong. The leaders were corrupt. The people were in distress. Violence had broken out everywhere. At the same time, God was rousing an enemy, a people called the Chaldeans. At first, they weren't much of an opponent, but over time they gained in strength, power, and evil. They became known for plundering and pillaging like pirates. And now, they were on the rampage, coming after Judah.

All seemed hopeless. A Chaldean invasion would mean devastation on so many fronts. No food. No money. No sustenance. No livelihood. Habakkuk was afraid.

This is so real. Loss, struggle, the fight against coming trouble. But we don't need to understand what God is doing in order to trust Him.

In the third chapter of this book, Habakkuk experienced a shift. He moved from a place of fear and worry to a place of deep trust: "Yet I will rejoice in the LORD! I will be joyful in the God of my salvation!" (v. 18 NLT).

What changed? Why did Habakkuk switch his song from worry to joy? It seems that his perspective shifted. Initially, all he could see was his enemy coming at him. But then it's as if he looked up and saw that his God was so much bigger than his enemy. While his enemy was a real threat, Habakkuk knew God was actually the one in control, and he chose to trust Him. This is something we're trying to teach our kids, and in teaching them, I'm teaching myself too. You have the choice to rejoice. You have the choice to enjoy a new

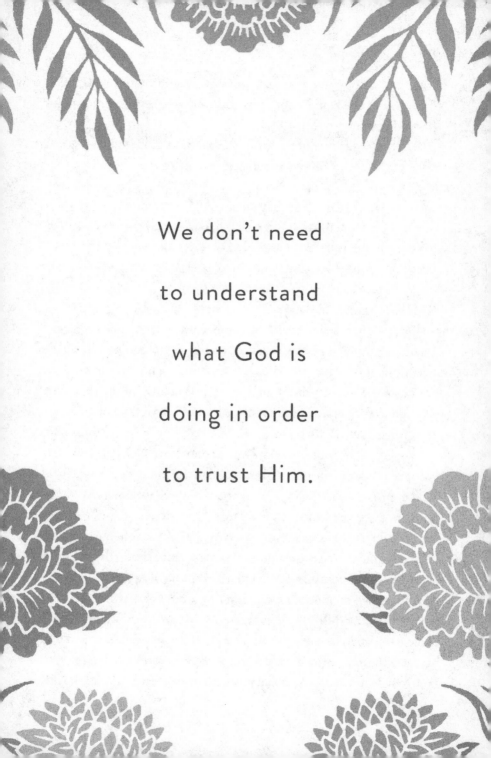

We don't need

to understand

what God is

doing in order

to trust Him.

route or a detour and not to let your circumstances define you. You can stick to the plan of choosing joy, even when the plan changes beyond your control.

In the beginning of this prayer, Habakkuk declared his knowledge of God, who He is, and what He's done in the past.

> I have heard all about you, LORD.
> I am filled with awe by your amazing works.
> In this time of our deep need,
> help us again as you did in years gone by. (3:2 NLT)

This bold statement defined how Habakkuk was going to respond to the trials he faced. Habakkuk's name means "one who embraces." He didn't know how the situation was going to end, and it didn't seem hopeful in the moment. But he chose to hold on to God, to embrace the One he didn't understand. He chose to say that even though darkness surrounded him, he would trust the Lord.

We are faced with this choice every day. The only way to combat fear or discomfort or uncertainty is to rejoice in the God of our salvation. To rejoice means to triumph, so in the middle of the struggle and confusion, we can boldly say that although we don't feel victorious or strong or flourishing, we trust God is triumphant. He loves us enough to not leave us alone in this heartache. When we allow a circumstance to take away our joy, we're letting it take the strength we need to keep pushing through, to keep showing up, and to keep ourselves aware of what God might be doing that we can't see.

Habakkuk didn't try to pretend that his problems weren't there. He saw them for what they were. He also remembered that God was greater than his problems. It's tempting to ignore our struggles, to push them away, or to stay super busy in order to avoid dealing with them. But when we choose to trust God, when we allow Him to fill our dark places with joy, we can face what comes our way head-on. We can look the trials dead in the face and simultaneously say to God, "Even though I don't understand, I will still trust You." This is how we rejoice in the things that are so hard for us to go through and how we find the strength to press in and not give up.

What Are You Going to Do About It?

In the movie *Million Dollar Baby*, Hilary Swank plays Maggie Fitzgerald, a young boxer who wants to make it big and provide a better life for her family. Professional boxing looks to be her ticket. She asks Frankie Dunn, played by Clint Eastwood, to train her. He is reluctant at first but finally agrees.

In one scene, Maggie just can't close the distance with her opponent. The other boxer gets in some clean shots, but Maggie's got nothing. At the end of that round, Maggie tells her coach, "She's tough, I can't go inside. I can't get close enough to hit her."

"You know why that is?" Frankie answers. "Cause she's a better fighter than you are, that's why. She's younger, she's stronger, and she's more experienced. Now, what are you gonna do about it?"

What are you gonna do about it?

What a good question. There will always be those who are better and stronger and younger and hotter than us. There will always be challenges to figure out. We will always have to battle our inner critics. And as long as we live on this earth, we will have to wage war against the Enemy, who wants to knock us out. We can take the easy route and give up, or we can change our minds about bolting from the hard stuff. We can put a little more effort into living through it, even when we want to back away slowly so we can run away as fast as we can.

Doing anything of great significance is never easy. In any endeavor to effect change, to help people, to not live a nominal life, we have to work hard. As the saying goes, "If it were easy, anyone could do it."

God doesn't call us to take the wide road, which would be way easier. He asks us to walk the narrow one—the one that includes loss, difficulty, pain, relational conflict, and uncertainty. But we're not alone. I'm so thankful Jesus not only did the hard things Himself, but He also did the hardest thing. He died for us and conquered death so we could live an abundant, full life. With Him, all we do is win.

After Maggie's coach asks her, "What are you going to do about it?" Maggie steps back into the ring. With a new determination and focus, she does what she has to do, and knocks her opponent out.

I ask you the same question: When your life gets flipped upside down, what are you going to do about it? Get back in the ring and trust God. It's scary, yes, but it's right where you're supposed to be.

6

Stick to the Plan

I tend to back out of things pretty easily. Raising four kids, leading a church with my husband, and traveling with the family can thrust my overwhelmed mode into the red zone. When I feel like I can't do what I thought I could do, my first response is, "Let's cancel."

I once heard someone say something like, "No one is in charge of your schedule but you. So if you have too much going on, you can do something about it." That's true. My problem is that I make an appointment but schedule it at a weird time or don't allot the correct amount of margin for it, and before I know it my day gets too full. (Hi. I'm Jennie. I'm in my late thirties, and I'm still figuring myself out.)

Throughout our marriage, as Levi and I have sought to make game plans for our relationship, parenting, budgeting, and everyday life, we often remind each other to "stick to the plan." This means we commit to going through with whatever we decided on originally. We don't deviate from the plan, especially when we're not feeling it.

Recently, I was preparing to take a trip to NYC to meet up with some friends and attend Hillsong's Colour Conference. Our family had just traveled the week before, and everything in me was saying,

Stay home. You're tired. You just got back home. Your kids need you. You have way too much going on right now to take another trip.

I texted Levi: "I'm having a really hard time with leaving again this week."

His immediate response: "Stick to the plan."

In that one phrase, I knew he was saying, "Jennie, don't back out on what God has for you this week. It's going to be special. He's going to use you. Plus, you get to spend time with friends you don't see often. Stick to the plan."

I needed to hear this. If Levi hadn't reminded and encouraged me to do the hard thing, I would have missed out on precious time spent with friends who also lead churches with their husbands. And I would have missed out on what God so clearly spoke to my heart through the conference and even in meeting new women who spoke such love and life over me.

Sticking to the plan is a great protocol to follow in all areas of life. Take marriage, for example: in the midst of heated moments, we can stick to the plan of loving and honoring our spouses, believing the best about them, and serving them even when we don't feel like it. This applies to the budget too: we can pull some Dave Ramsey–esque ninja moves and stick to our planned spending. As he would say, "Live like no one else now, so you can live like no one else later."

Getting to the Other Side

You might be thinking, *Sticking to the plan is great in theory, Jennie, but what about giving God space to do something different and change up our plans?* Great point! I'm so glad you brought it up.

When we give our lives to God, we surrender to Him what we

think we want and allow Him to lead us. But we also pray and plan and prepare. We know that we can do our part, but ultimately we're giving God the override button so He can do whatever He wants to do in and through us.

As Proverbs 16:9 says, "A man's heart plans his way, but the LORD directs his steps." We plan; He pilots. We schedule; He gets the final say. So when I say "stick to the plan," I mean *stick to the plan of trusting God with our lives* and doing what He asks us to do. If He changes things up, we continue to stick to the plan of trusting and obeying Him, no matter how we feel.

Every January before my birthday, I choose a passage or chapter in the book of Psalms or Proverbs as my anthem for that year. In 2019, I picked Psalm 37. Here's part of it: "Trust in the LORD, and do good; dwell in the land, and feed on His faithfulness. Delight yourself also in the LORD, and He shall give you the desires of your heart. Commit your way to the LORD, trust also in Him, and He shall bring it to pass" (vv. 3–5).

The best way to start sticking to the plan is to trust in the Lord. This is God we're talking about here: the fashion designer of the universe, of the world, of you and me. The Bible says of Him:

Have you not known?
>Have you not heard?
>The everlasting God, the LORD,
>The Creator of the ends of the earth,
>Neither faints nor is weary.
>His understanding is unsearchable.
>He gives power to the weak,
>And to those who have no might He increases strength.
>(Isaiah 40:28–29)

God is trustworthy. We can delight in and commit our way to Him, and He will do the beautiful things that He wants to do in us and through us. We experience peace and confidence when we stick to the plan, even if it's one that God knows and we don't. This takes away the pressure of trying to be in control and to figure it all out.

After Jesus spent a day teaching by the Sea of Galilee, He turned to his disciples and said, "Okay, guys, let's hop in this boat. We're going to the other side" (Mark 4:35, my paraphrase). Jesus told them the plan, and the disciples climbed in. Not long after, a storm came in. Waves lashed over the boat, and it began taking on water. The disciples started panicking. This was definitely not part of the plan.

And where was Jesus? Asleep in the stern. (When you've been working hard and you have a minute for a nap, don't ask any questions—just take it.) When the disciples shook Him awake, I imagine He looked at them and sighed. "You guys. Some of you are professional fishermen. Don't you know this lake by now?" It's true. Technically, the ones who were fishermen should have known that this body of water was often susceptible to sudden storms. More than that, they seemed to forget—or didn't realize—who was in charge of the lake.

After Jesus rebuked the wind and told the raging waters to be still, He turned to the disciples and said, "Why are you so fearful? How is it that you have no faith?" (Mark 4:40). Jesus' plan was to get to the other side. That's what was going to happen, regardless of the storm.

I love what Charlotte Gambill says about this in her book *The Miracle in the Middle:* "The turbulence we face does not alter the instructions He sends . . . it is in the middle of the storm that we discover what is in the middle of us."

The intensity of a trial or a challenge shouldn't change our

The intensity of a

trial or a challenge

shouldn't change

our obedience

to the plan God

laid out for us.

obedience to the plan God laid out for us. This is true even if it's hard, even if the plan doesn't make any sense or makes us feel confused or angry or sad. The big question is, will we trust Him?

If He says we're going to the other side, that's exactly what we are going to do.

Who's in Charge Around Here?

I've struggled my whole life with letting my emotions be the boss of me. I still have my very first journal, which my parents gave me when I was eight. So many entries talked about how mad someone made me, or how I hated this person and was bugged by that person. I read it to my daughters recently, and we all had a good laugh at my issues as an eight-year-old. Over the years, these anger issues turned into other emotional struggles. I was a mess. I still am, but thankfully I've learned a few things since then.

(I'm going to pause for a sec and tell you that my husband wrote a book called *I Declare War* about this very subject. In this book, Levi talks about declaring war on the one who can do the most damage to us: ourselves. This book was so much what I needed that I sometimes wonder if he wrote it as a result of being married to me. If you haven't yet, go ahead and buy it now. I promise it will change your life. Okay, end of shameless plug.)

I love the movie *Southpaw*. It's about boxing, but it's also a film that has made me want to be a better wife because of how the main character's wife encourages and champions her husband. Jake Gyllenhaal plays Billy Hope, a champion boxer at the end of his career. His anger motivates his fighting, and it's what he uses in the ring to beat his opponents.

At the beginning of the movie, Billy is in a downward spiral, little by little losing everything that matters in his life. He gets into a street fight with a younger, stronger boxer. Billy's wife, who encourages her husband to let go of the conflict and go home, gets shot in the crossfire and dies. At this point, everything changes for Billy. He tries to get revenge by hunting down the guy who shot his wife. Then, as his anger and grief grow out of control, Billy tries to kill himself in a car accident. But even this isn't his lowest point. When he tries to punch a referee after losing a fight, Billy's career is over. And when he is declared an unfit parent, the state intervenes and takes his daughter into custody. This is Billy's biggest blow, and the one that finally forces him to come to his senses.

Billy finds a new coach, Tick Wills, played by Forest Whitaker. The boxer sobers up and starts to train again. I'll never forget one scene between Billy and Tick. Tick tells him, "The way you fight, anger's your biggest tool. Fighting angry, that drains you twice as fast. The other guy in the ring is your enemy, but if all you're trying to do is kill him, then you expose yourself. You leave yourself vulnerable."

It's easy to let the angry monster or the negative monster or the bitter monster or the frustrated monster inside us bust out in all its raging glory. It's much harder to choose to let God's love lead. To let kindness be the boss. To communicate what's frustrating and try to see the situation from the other person's perspective. To stick to the bigger plan of loving God and loving others instead of being led by our feelings or our circumstances.

It's easy to stay stuck in our pain or to blame what happened to us on the parents we had or the ones we didn't have as a way of saying, "I'm this way because I've had a hard life." Our experiences are definitely a part of who we are and who we become, but using them as an excuse to engage in bad behaviors will keep us from growing. When we do this, we short circuit God's plan for us to live the flourishing lives we were designed to live.

At times it's still hard for me to navigate a disagreement without letting my emotions and feelings lead. But I've learned that I can fight fair without letting anger or hurt be my motivation. I'm able to communicate and say how I feel without losing my temper. I'm able to grow in this process and, as a result, so do my relationships.

What Story Are You Telling?

Emotions are good. God gave them to us. They prove that we're human and that we feel. But instead of allowing them to overpower us, we can say, "Hey, anger" or "Hey, feelings, I totally feel you, but who do you think you are? You can't drive. That's my job. Get back in the passenger seat."

In her book *Rising Strong*, Brené Brown offered advice on how to be better understood, which makes for creating strong and healthy relationships. She wrote, "If I could give men and women in relationship and leaders and parents one hack, I would give them, 'the story I'm making up.' . . . Basically, you're telling the other person your reading of the situation—and simultaneously admitting that you know it can't be 100% accurate."

Brené gave a great example of this principle in action. She wrote about taking a swim with her husband on vacation. At one point, she looked at him and said something sweet. She was hoping for a romantic reply, but it never came. Brené felt embarrassed and tried again. Her husband gave another equally dull response. She wrote, "All I knew was that I had already scripted the rest of the morning on the swim back, and without an intervention we were headed toward a terrible day."

Instead of lashing out in anger at his failure to respond with sweetness, Brené opted for kindness. She told her husband about the story she was making up: that she was getting old, that she didn't look as hot in her swimsuit as she used to. As it turned out, he had no idea what she was saying in the first place. The night before he'd had a dream about their kids almost drowning. The only thing on his mind in the water that day was that nightmare.

Sorting through the story in my head during difficult situations in my marriage hasn't been easy. It doesn't come naturally, particularly if I'm feeling misunderstood or hurt or exhausted. But everything changes when I don't respond immediately with anger, and I give myself the space, even a few seconds, to not assume the story is what I think it is.

Out of My Feelings

In an argument with Levi, I usually feel comfortable staying in my feelings. I don't want to budge because my feelings are good company. They tell me what I want to hear. But when I can express my feelings and see the truth of a situation—like that I'm not meant to fight *against* Levi or my kids but *with* and *for* them—I gain a clearer perspective.

When I take a moment to think about what's really going on in a situation, I can choose to not give my feelings final say over me. Levi and I are on the same team; we're meant to fight against our own self-interest and to put each other's needs before our own. I have to remember the endgame, the purpose and plan of what God has called us to. I have to choose to allow His Word, not how I feel, to lead me.

When the kids fight and I'm disengaged, focusing on something else, my first response always comes from a place of frustration because I'm distracted. I expect them to treat each other with kindness, but I'm also supposed to help them by modeling this behavior. Instead of jumping into their fight harshly, the best thing to do is to put aside whatever I am doing, be present in the situation, and bring the intensity down by being calm myself. That said, I don't always succeed in controlling my emotions. In particular, I have regrets about disciplining Lenya. She was a sweetheart and also a stubborn stinker and knew just how to push my buttons. She would often scream and yell. There were many times I corrected her behavior harshly—and that's never okay.

I remember weeping in the shower about a month after Lenya went to heaven, feeling the weight of what kind of parent I was to her. I was a good mom, but I also was not. I'm guessing many moms feel that way. (One of the things Lenya told me often when I was disciplining her was "You're a bad mommy!" or "You're the worst mommy in the world!" But five minutes later she'd say, "I love you, Mommy! You're the best mommy in the world!" Why do the wild emotions of a five-year-old feel so relatable as an adult?) I know at times I was impatient, not understanding, and too rigid. But in the last few months of Lenya's life, I felt like I was coming to understand her and figuring out how to best parent her.

As the water splashed over me in the shower that morning, tears streamed down my face. I was heartbroken I wouldn't get the chance to keep growing with her. I wrote in my journal later:

There's a deep ache in my soul. I miss the Lenya Benya. I really need to watch my attitude though. To really allow myself to focus on heaven, on eternity, and not get caught up in my feelings and regrets.

I regret so many things, not being more understanding of her and her cute personality, not listening to her on the day she went to heaven, not snuggling her more closely, not cherishing her more dearly. But God, YOU are faithful and all-knowing, and I thank You that You're using this to humble me and break me down. To be a better mother. To be a more loving/ understanding mother. To cherish and to love more deeply. I love You, Lord.

I'm reminded of words lovingly spoken by my friend Lysa TerKeurst that have helped me so much. During a Q&A on our tour, she said, "Bad moments don't make bad moms." There's grace in this mess, and there's hope in the mistakes we make.

Just Breathe

If you remember anything from science class in elementary school, you know that plants take in water, carbon dioxide, and sunlight to make glucose and oxygen. I'm talking, of course, about photosynthesis. Did you also know that although plants don't have lungs or a bloodstream like we do, they release oxygen and absorb carbon dioxide from the air? In other words, they breathe.

Over the years, I've learned the importance of pausing, taking a deep breath, and thinking through my response. Taking a moment to think, even when it means stepping into another room, has helped. It's like I need a quick time-out before I give one. When I use that space to breathe and to calm my emotions, I can refocus and take a better approach. It helps to take my feelings out of the situation and see the bigger picture. I can stick to the plan of teaching my children effectively—not just telling them in the moment how to act but showing them in a critical moment how to live.

Right before I put Lennox down in his crib for the night, I hold him tight. He immediately rests his head on my right shoulder. This is usually a moment for me to catch my breath before the evening ends and I start preparing the younger girls for bed. One night I took a deep breath and he copied me right away, breathing in and out. Since then, every night, we take deep breaths together. Sometimes he does it before me. My little boy unknowingly reminds me to slow down.

Breathing is, for the most part, an unconscious action. We inhale oxygen, which creates energy, and exhale carbon dioxide. When we breathe deeply, with intention, we increase the amount of oxygen in our blood more than we do when breathing naturally. The brain senses this increase in oxygen and decreases the amount of stress hormones in the blood. Conversely, taking short breaths increases our unease. Our bodies clench tighter and prevent us from relaxing.

There's actually strength in breathing deeply, especially in such a physically intense activity like boxing. I read that "breathing correctly when throwing punches helps add power to your punches, keeps your lungs full of oxygen and prevents you from overtiring." Breathing the right way, while working out and in life, keeps us from losing focus. If we can learn to breathe properly, we'll be able to live powerfully.

Deep breathing has been a game changer for me. I have to be intentional and think about it to do it. When I do, I'm able to step out of my emotions and ask God for His strength and grace. And then I'm reminded to stick to the plan.

When we stick to

the plan of trusting

God, He can help

us change our

hearts, even when

our emotions try

to take us in the

opposite direction.

When we stick to the plan of trusting God, He can help us change our hearts, even when our emotions try to take us in the opposite direction. After all, we live by faith, not by sight—and certainly not by our feelings.

Champagne and Cookies

As I was writing this, alone in my hotel room, someone knocked on my door. A voice on the other side announced cheerfully, "Room service!" Weird—I hadn't ordered anything. I opened the door, and a man in a hotel uniform told me management wanted to give me champagne and cookies. In his outstretched hands was a silver tray piled with the most delicious-looking cookies I'd ever seen and a bottle of golden bubbly.

The thing is, I was currently in the middle of a twenty-one-day fast where I was abstaining from certain foods. How easy would it have been to say yes and not stick to the plan? Very easy. The author of Psalm 73:26 tells us, "My flesh and my heart fail; but God is the strength of my heart and my portion forever." We are weak. We cave in. We fail. We let our feelings get the best of us. But God is the One who gives us the strength we need and the One who sustains us. Our confidence in Him helps us stick to His plan for us.

We don't have to fall for the champagne and cookies. We don't have to say yes to whatever we feel. With God, we can stick to the plan.

When you fall short, look up. You can't change what happened or how you messed up. Remind yourself that God "gives power to the weak, and to those who have no might He increases strength. Even the youths shall faint and be weary, and the young men shall utterly fall, but those who wait on the LORD shall renew their strength; they shall mount up with wings like eagles, they shall run and not be weary, they shall walk and not faint" (Isaiah 40:29–31).

There's renewed strength waiting for you. There's so much more around the corner. And while there's more pain and heartache to come, there's also more joy and more beauty than you could ever have thought possible.

7

Embrace the Beauty in the Blend

If you have some time to waste, search for "Will it blend?" on Google. You'll find a man named Tom Dickson, founder of Blendtec, the manufacturer of what the company claims is the most advanced blender. As zany music plays in the background, Tom starts off one of many videos by asking, "Will it blend? That is the question!" He goes on to place random objects, like an iPhone, golf balls, or superglue, in a blender to see if the item will indeed blend. It's crazy and cheesy, but it's also pretty awesome.

I've found that the hard parts and the good parts of life don't happen separately; they usually happen simultaneously. We can experience mountaintop highs and valley lows at the exact same time, and in a way they blend together. It doesn't seem possible, but the sooner we can recognize and embrace the fact that there's beauty in the blend, the sooner we can live through it confidently and with purpose.

In the Bible, when Job was dealing with one tragedy after another, his wife told him that he should just curse God and die. Wow. What a way to live your life, Job's wife! No encouragement, no trying to find the silver lining; just a "Give up, Job. Throw in the towel and die" (Job 2:9, my paraphrase). But look at Job's response, which is so good: "You speak as one of the foolish women speaks. Shall we indeed accept good from God, and shall we not accept adversity?" (v. 10). How wise was Job?

Let's take this a step further. How can we be certain a given situation is good or bad? I heard someone say that sometimes going through a bad situation can have a more positive impact than going through a good situation.

Sure, horrible (and evil) things fog up this world—like racism, shootings, rape, murder, kidnapping, and sex trafficking, to name a few. Yes, I am labeling them as bad. God does too. He hates these things with a capital *H*. In fact, Jesus even said that if anyone hurts the little ones who believe in Him, it would be better for them if a cement block was tied to their necks and they were thrown into the ocean (Mark 9:42).

God hates injustice and evil and abuse. But because we live in an imperfect world full of sin and full of people who need to know how much God loves them, these atrocities will be with us until we reach heaven. So what do we do? If we can dare to see the way God sees, how He tucks good inside the bad, we can change how we are affected by these things. God doesn't make evil things happen, but He is the Redeemer and the Restorer of everything. He is the One who makes all things new, even if it means making us new in the midst of the pain done to us or the pain we have caused.

Jesus said that if we have faith even as small as a tiny mustard seed, we can say to a huge mountain to throw itself from here to there (Matthew 17:20). But my husband has pointed out, "Sometimes the mountain that is moved is the one inside of you." Levi is suggesting that perhaps it's the mountain of our sin, or our pain, or our wounds, or our heartache, or our pride that needs to be moved.

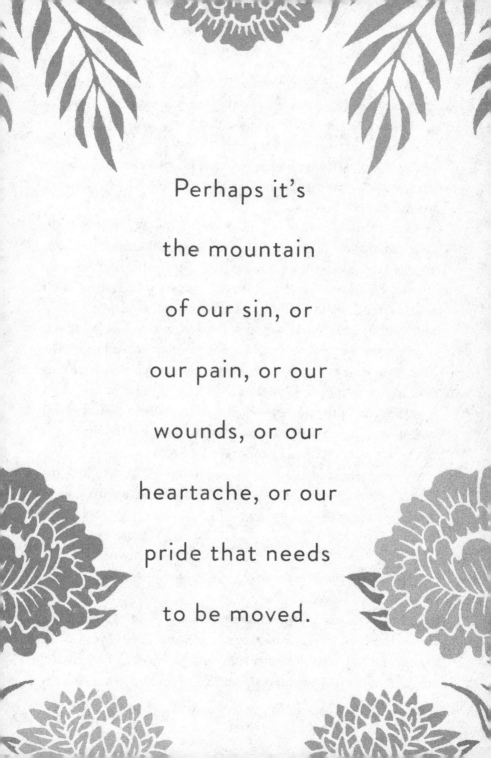

Perhaps it's

the mountain

of our sin, or

our pain, or our

wounds, or our

heartache, or our

pride that needs

to be moved.

My dear friend Katherine Wolf suffered a massive stroke at age twenty-six. In an extensive sixteen-hour brain surgery, over half of Katherine's cerebellum was removed. Miraculously, she survived the surgery, but her nervous system was severely compromised. Since the stroke, Katherine has relearned how to eat, talk, and walk. Today, much of the right side of her body is impaired, and she relies greatly on her wheelchair.

I love what she said in an interview: "Suffering is the common denominator in our humanity and points us to Jesus, and so I want to instill in my kids the notion that hard and good are not mutually exclusive to each other—that things can be very good and very hard at the same time." Katherine and her husband, Jay, could have let this confusing and debilitating life they had been handed knock them out of the ring, but they decided to choose daily to see their lives from God's vantage point. They continue to choose to see the whole picture, the good and the devastating mixed together.

Katherine calls the wheelchair she sits in every day her "seat of honor." I have never heard anyone define what confines them as their calling, but Katherine does. She and Jay inspire me to change my perspective of what I call *good* and what I call *bad*. In both the small, daily struggles and in the bigger trials, I want to find the good in the difficulty, the beauty in the blend.

Rainbow Waterfalls

Each of my children has a different relationship with Lenya. Alivia remembers her; they were best friends. When Lenya went to heaven, Daisy and Clover were two and one, so their memory of her is not that strong. Levi, Alivia, and I love telling the girls about their sister who is waiting for them in heaven. It has been so hard to see them grieve differently at different ages over the years. Alivia will plainly say, "I'm so sad Lenya's not here." Daisy has said many times, "I miss Lenya." Clover will come up to me crying and say, "I'm sad I didn't know Lenya. I wish she was here. Tell me about her." When I was pregnant with Lennox, the girls began talking and scheming how they would tell their little brother about his big sister in heaven. Recently, two-year-old Lennox asked me, "Watch Lenya shows?"

Watching videos and thumbing through photo books of Lenya help them feel like they know her and that she's not far away.

It has been important for our family to find special ways to celebrate Lenya on her birthday and on the day she arrived in heaven. Because we have little ones, Levi and I want to celebrate in a way that is fun for them.

It happened by accident, but the first anniversary of Lenya's heaven homecoming ended up being a day full of color. In the winter, our daughter's grave is covered in snow, and the little vase connected to her gravestone is frozen, so we can't put flowers in it. That morning, on a random Target run, Levi had found snow paint. I didn't even know such a thing existed. You fill a big, squeezable tube with water, dissolve a colored tablet in it, then splash it across the snow as you would when pouring flavored syrup on a snow cone. My husband came home with the idea of painting Lenya's grave later that day. It was such an amazing idea. (Good one, Levi Aaron Lusko!)

Through tears, I watched Alivia, Daisy, and Clover, "paintbrushes" in hand, make a colorful masterpiece all around Lenya's snowy grave. Our miniature Picassos painted flowers and hearts, anchors and smiley faces, scribbles (Clover's work of art), and Lenya's name. Splashes of bright red, blue, purple, pink, and yellow spilled in beautiful mayhem all over the white canvas. We blew kisses to heaven and drove away. It was special and terrible, all mixed together.

Later, we drove to Hungry Horse Dam to look for frozen waterfalls. Much to our amazement, we stumbled upon one that had been painted to look like a rainbow. I don't know how the artist did it, but the cascade of icicles were covered in color. I think the girls thought it was naturally like that. We took pictures in front of this breathtaking work of art—it was so magical. This was the start of making Lenya's special days full of color and vibrancy.

We ended that day watching videos of Lenya we had never seen. They were like gold at the end of a rainbow. (If you have pictures or videos of people who are no longer with you, text them or send copies to their family—it's like a treasure.) In one video, Lenya is wearing a Snow White costume for no reason except that's what Lenya did. Every day was dress-up day. In dramatic fashion, she lays down on the ground and says, "I will die like this and wake up with Jesus and be in heaven!"

Levi and I wept, dumbfounded. The video was taken five days before Lenya went to heaven.

We replayed it over and over again. It gave me great comfort to know our daughter declared her faith so strongly just days before arriving in heaven.

After we laughed and cried while watching videos of our little lion, Alivia asked to watch the memorial service, which included a video collage of Lenya that our friend and worship pastor, Kevin, had labored over and created specifically for us. There Lenya was, dancing in one of her mismatched outfits with her sisters. Then, a scene of her trying to catch the incoming tide on a beach with Alivia. In other moments, she twirled in a ballet recital, ran barefoot in the grass, and recited Psalm 23 in her adorable, raspy three-year-old little voice. Cue the tears.

In the thick fog of grief, there were still faint whispers of hope. A few days later, on January 8, 2014, I wrote:

A new day.

Lord, I really feel like I've been in a new season of healing. And I know a wave will hit me every now and again, but overall, I feel like there has been a change in my heart. My soul still aches, but there's just so much peace. When I think about that night there's deep pain, but then I remember Who she is with. I remember that I will see Lenya soon. Sooner than I think.

And Lord, You have been so faithful to carry me, yet protect me, and all at the same time lead me. And I want to keep running hard, to love sacrificially, to honor relentlessly, to give cheerfully.

Mourning and Dancing

No matter how much fun we plan on Lenya's special days, there's always a void. The beauty of nature, playful balloons, a dance party, or the magic of rainbow-colored snow doesn't mask the reality that Lenya isn't here. There's an underlying tension between celebrating her life and recognizing her absence. I call it *happysad*. Yes, I know I can't go around making up my own words, but it's all I can say sometimes. When a friend moves away and isn't in my life anymore, I'm happysad. I'm happy for her future but sad we're not together anymore.

There's a purpose

in our pain: to

speak and sing

of who He is and

not be silent.

Psalm 30:11–12 says, "You have turned my mourning into joyful dancing. You have taken away my clothes of mourning and clothed me with joy, that I might sing praises to you and not be silent. O LORD my God, I will give you thanks forever!" (NLT).

Did you catch that? He clothes us with joy *so that* we can sing praises and not be silent. There's a purpose in our pain: to speak and sing of who He is and not be silent. This joy is possible for all of us who have experienced any kind of loss. God doesn't give us the fullness of His joy by completely removing the heartache. We're not in heaven yet, where there are no tears and no pain. We are here on earth, and so we have both joy and hardship, peace and trouble, midnight and dawn.

The night of Lenya's celebration of life, we invited family and friends over to a nearby lodge where we played music and set up a candy buffet for the kids (okay—for the adults too). In the midst of the shock and ache, I remember standing, numb, talking with Chris and Tatum Norman, friends who had traveled from California to be with us. Alivia came up to me with a Shirley Temple she had made for me. I remember looking across the room and seeing a bunch of little kids dancing to the music. Dancing and mourning.

Recently, Levi and I were in Florida. We got up super early one morning, way before the first moment of light. The two of us sat on the balcony of our hotel room, staring out into the ocean. The sky and water were dark. Ever so softly, dawn broke, and with it came light. As the sun began to rise over the horizon, bursts of gold and crimson and deep purple scattered across the sky. The color display was incredible. I tried to snap a picture of it but obviously could not do the scene justice. Once the sun had fully entered the sky, it was super bright—almost blinding. I made a mental note that the most beautiful moment of color was right at dawn.

That sunrise was such a picture to me of how on this side of heaven, we will always walk in darkness and light. Jesus is the Light of the World, and as we live in Him and endure painful moments, we will still experience opportunities for beauty. It may not feel like it, it may not seem like it, but they're there.

Some species of plants can thrive in poor soil because of an unlikely partnership—bacteria. I know, talk about a mismatched couple. But bacteria can actually enrich nutrient-deficient soil for the plant so it grows properly. We cannot avoid the bad things that happen in life, but we can ask God to open our eyes to see how the good and the bad blend. We can even ask Him to help us see that we need the hard things in order to flourish.

Black and White, and Color All Over

Color changes our perspective.

As I was in the early stages of working on this book, we celebrated what would have been Lenya's eleventh birthday on September 8, 2018. On that same day, our city was hosting a color run. Participants wear white, but their clothes don't stay that way for very long. During and after the five-kilometer run, people are splashed with colored powder from head to toe. It's wild and messy and bright and amazing. I thought it would be fun to gather a few friends and family to run together in this color fest.

I started the day instructing a spin class, using a playlist I created that included some of Lenya's favorite songs. Right after, I met up with everyone at the color run. My daughters and I handed out rainbow-colored sweatbands and heart-shaped sunglasses for friends and family to wear. The day ended in a crescendo with our

Fresh Life worship experience. It was like a celebratory triathlon—spin/run/church—for our little lion. Levi preached that night, so it was more like a triathlon plus a marathon for him.

That night, the six of us cuddled on the couch. Levi turned on the video of the memorial service. I lost it. I sobbed more than I had in a long time. Six years had passed since I'd held Lenya in my arms, but right then, the wound was fresh, as if only yesterday her tiny five-year-old hand was wrapped in mine.

This part of the healing process feels unending. Grief comes in waves; everybody tells you this. No matter how many times I've watched this video, I weep. I don't mind. I hope there is never a day that I watch Lenya's video and don't cry. Every time the hurt of my heart reopens, it's an opportunity for God to continue to heal me. He allows me to see the opening in the fog. He adds color to the black-and-white story of my life that continues to unfold. And He reminds me that fighting and flourishing are meant to blend.

8

Right Here, Right Now

Three nights before Lenya went to heaven, Levi and I were attending one of our many events scheduled for that week while my sister Chelsea watched our kids. When we came home, they were asleep, so she and I sat on the couch for some sister time. In the middle of our conversation, I heard someone coming down the stairs. I knew it was Lenya by the cadence of her steps.

She crept toward the living room with as much sneakiness as she could and sidled up next to me. "Mom, I want you to come upstairs," she whined.

A pro at combating bedtime battles, I knew the drill. I looked her in the eyes and calmly but firmly said, "Lenya, I'm talking with Auntie Chelsea. It's time to go back upstairs and to bed." She just stood there as if I hadn't said a word.

"Lenya, it's late. You need to go back to bed," I repeated, this time with a little more intensity. Lenya wasn't having it. Finally, I got off the couch, picked her up, and carried her to the stairs.

If I remember correctly, Lenya told me, "But I'm scared. There's something in my room. I want you with me." As I think about that right now, tears fill my eyes and an ache of regret fills my heart. Why didn't I take that moment to be with her? Why didn't I press Pause on my conversation with Chelsea and take five minutes to lie down and pray with my daughter? Looking back, I wish I had handled the situation differently.

Parents experience such a tension between fighting for structure and taking time to engage. The line can be blurry. Kids have to go to bed; they need sleep. If you have children and they're anything like mine, you know a simple fifteen-minute bedtime routine can easily turn into a two-hour bombardment of requests—anything to delay the inevitable:

"I want a sip of water."

"I forgot my blankie."

"I need to go to the bathroom."

"I just want to snuggle you."

That last one always gets me, especially when my kids say it with that innocent look in their eyes. I know that children thrive in a loving environment that includes structure, rules, and boundaries. At the same time, I want to always be sensitive to the Holy Spirit and correctly interpret whether what my children are asking is a delay tactic or if they really need me.

Levi once preached on the importance of being childlike, not childish. One of the things he said was that we should take time to listen to our kids, because there's so much we can learn from them. They can offer great wisdom because of their simple perspectives. Jesus said, "Beware that you don't look down on any of these little ones. For I tell you that in heaven their angels are always in the presence of my heavenly Father" (Matthew 18:10 NLT). I love this verse because Jesus condemned people who regarded little ones as insignificant. Here, He also mentioned that children have angels assigned to them. Isn't that amazing? Clover and Lennox probably have thirty angels between the two of them because they are constantly falling, hitting their heads, and getting hurt. When we get to heaven, our bill for these angels is going to be through the roof.

Speaking of angels, Jesus also talked about a poor man who died and was accompanied by an angel to heaven (Luke 16:22). I think back on the night Lenya said, "I want you with me," and wonder what she was dealing with. She was so close to seeing Jesus. Maybe there really was something in her room. Maybe it was an angel and its presence frightened her. I won't know the answer this side of heaven, although I wish I could. But through this and many other instances, God has been teaching me to allow the Holy Spirit to impress on my heart when to release my agenda and take a second. To lay down my task-oriented mind and to engage in the moment. To snuggle. To listen. To practice tenderness.

One of the things I love about Jesus is that He always took time with people, no matter how busy He was. We get to see so many of these examples throughout the Gospels, but the story of Zacchaeus stands out to me. Luke 19 begins with the statement that Jesus was passing through Jericho. It wasn't His destination; He was just passing through. A rich tax collector named Zacchaeus lived there and wanted to see Jesus. In those days, tax collectors were known for taking from people more than was necessary. They stole to become rich.

As much as Zacchaeus wanted to see Jesus, he had a problem. He was short, so he wouldn't have been able to get Jesus' attention in a crowd. This didn't stop him. Zacchaeus ran ahead of the crowd and climbed a tree to get a better view. That took effort on Zacchaeus's part! He didn't know Jesus, but he ran *and* climbed a tree to see Him, neither of which were easy. When Jesus walked by and looked up, he told Zacchaeus to get down because he was coming over to his house (vv. 3–5).

It's hard to compare ourselves to Jesus, because He is God and He knows exactly how to read people and handle even the stickiest of situations. But this doesn't mean we can't learn to do what He did and live how He lived. Each day, we can ask God to open our eyes to the people He wants us to take a moment with—the people he wants us to notice, to love, to encourage, to be there for, and to invite ourselves over for dinner with (okay, maybe not so much that one)—right here, right now.

Undivided Attention

On one hand, I live very much in the moment. On the other hand, I live very much *not* in the moment. This is evident in simple ways. I'll be reading a story to my kids, but my mind is somewhere else. I'm thinking about what happened that morning or about the meeting I still need to plan for the next day. I have to fight hard to focus.

One of my favorite things I've heard instructors say in a spin class or boxing class is "Be here now. Don't think about the next thing. Be present. Focus. Let's work hard and get the most out of these forty-five minutes." *Be here now.* Right here, right now. Don't worry about the next thing, but pour the most into and get the most out of the present moment. This kind of living will bring beauty and significance into our daily lives.

My prayer for a long time has been *God, help me to listen. Help me to be aware. Help me to engage.* To engage means to "occupy oneself or become involved." When you're thinking about a hundred different things, you can't fully be in the moment. You can't give your undivided attention when your attention is divided. I've learned the hard way how important it is. It's something I'm still growing in, so I'll let you in on my process and progress.

Each year, we encourage the people in our church to pick a word or two that they believe God is speaking over them and that they want to grow in that particular year. In 2019, the word for me was *immerse*, which means "to involve deeply, to absorb." In a practical sense, the word meant that this year I would put my whole heart into whatever I was doing.

One of the many things I love about Levi is that he is immersive—all-in with everything. When we were trying to find a stroller and a car seat for Lennox, this man lived and breathed strollers and car seats for weeks. He researched and pored over YouTube reviews every day until he found the perfect ones. Levi prepares his weekend messages with the same intensity. After diving into the material and asking questions, he likes to process his thoughts outwardly. I've come to realize the importance of diving into this part of the process with him.

I had a minor surgery at the end of 2018. While I was recovering and limited physically, I had to figure out the schedule for the week, who was going to be with the kids, who was going to help with laundry, what things I needed to do now and what could wait. I was in the zone when Levi, who had been studying, came bounding down the stairs. Excited and without missing a beat, he looked at me and said, "Okay, so here's what I'm thinking about my message. Tell me what you think." As he shared what was on his heart for our church, I had to force myself to be present and engage with his way of processing. I had to step away from *manage-my-life* mode and power on the *I'm-here-and-listening-to-you* mode. It's a huge deal for Levi to let me into his world. I don't want to half-listen and not give him the best of me in that moment. I want to focus and immerse myself fully, to listen and affirm him and give my undivided attention.

I'm so thankful that God is patient and faithful with me. Sometimes after similar moments with Levi, I've left the conversation kicking myself because I was *so* not in the moment. I could have been more encouraging or given better feedback. If I'm called to be Levi's wife, then I am also meant to be his greatest fan, coach, and cheerleader. My failures are many, but I can see how over the last few years God has helped me gain traction in this area. It's so encouraging when you fight to do the right thing and see glimpses of progress. The match may be long, but knowing I've won a round inspires me to fight harder and win the next one.

There Are No Shortcuts

We travel often, and coming home, I tend to be the worst version of me. I'm done dealing with airports, airplanes, bathrooms, feeling nauseous, and keeping Lennox from licking things. I just want to be home already.

I remember arriving at the airport once, when Clover, tired and homesick, looked at me and said, "Mom, I don't want to fly home. I just want to *be* home."

"Oh, Clover," I said with a sigh. "Me too, sweetie." I related to her more than she knew.

As she said this, I was reminded how there are no shortcuts to heaven, no shortcuts through life, no shortcuts through pain, and no shortcuts to becoming the beautiful picture on the seed packet of the flourishing woman that God has created each of us to be. Just as we have to go to the airport and through security to fly the last leg home, we have to go through the process of living on this road on our way to heaven. There's no secret passageway; we have to go through to get home.

When Levi and I introduced our kids to *Super Mario Bros*, we were so excited to show them the video games of our childhood. We showed them the secret blocks that would produce coins, and the rainbow flowers that would give an extra boost of superpower. We also showed them the ways to skip levels within the game. For example, as you finish the first level, there's a point where you can jump up, run across the highest ledge, and end up in a zone where you have the option to skip levels two, three, and four. #EightiesNerdsAlert

Have you ever wanted to rush through a time in your life to get to the next level? To avoid this heartache, this inconvenience, this pain, and magically end up somewhere easier, less demanding, and less overwhelming? We want to skip over the hard stuff; it's as though we're doing sit-ups in PE and stop the moment the coach turns her back, only to act like we were doing them all along when she turns around again. (I'm not necessarily speaking from experience. Okay, fine—I did this last week in a spin class during the arm workout.)

When we skip over the work God has for us, we shortchange ourselves. We get to the next season but without the tools, extra points, and spare lives we need to stay there. When you immerse yourself in where you are right now, God will give you the ability to push through. It's in this tension that we grow.

As a woman, and especially as a mother, I find that it's so easy to get bogged down by the little details of everyday life. We can let daily living become dull and keep us from taking a moment to look up and see the beauty around us. We see the negative, not the wonder. We see the blinding brightness of the sun, not the beauty

When you immerse
yourself in where
you are right
now, God will give
you the ability
to push through.
It's in this tension
that we grow.

of the sunset. We see the work we have to endure, not the life we get to live. We see the aches and pains, not the opportunities to be the light God designed us to be.

In his book *A Long Obedience in the Same Direction*, Eugene Peterson wrote about traveling the long road of discipleship with Jesus. He taught how to grow daily in purpose, passion, worship, prayer, joy, and community. The book's theme is based on a quote from Friedrich Nietzsche: "The essential thing 'in heaven and earth' is . . . that there should be a long obedience in the same direction; there thereby results, and has always resulted in the long run, something which has made life worth living."

When I think of "a long obedience in the same direction," I think about fighting for the seemingly insignificant details that fill a day. Being fully immersed and consistent in the little things. Being committed to the long haul, rising up in strength and honor, and embracing the daily grind with all of my heart. I think of finding purpose in moments big and small; looking for beauty in a mess, growth in a trial; gaining a deeper perspective of what may seem frustrating or annoying.

It's (Not) Just a Table

A few years ago, I was putting dishes away when I tripped, for probably the five-hundredth time, over a small table. My first reaction was to think how glad I would be when it was finally gone, not in the center of the kitchen.

Then I stopped myself in the middle of my selfish and whiny tracks. *No*, I said to myself. *I'll actually be really sad when it's time for this tiny piece of furniture to be thrown out.*

It was just a little brown table. The paint was chipping away. It was missing a chair. It usually had something sticky on it. Overall, it was a very unimpressive thing.

But I realized at that moment how special this table really was—not because of the table itself but because of the little girls who have sat around it over the years. This square table had been a breakfast and lunch restaurant, a place for royalty during tea parties, and creation central for paintings and collages and other works of art. It's been a table where little girls have learned to sit like ladies, where they have engaged in some of the most imaginative conversations.

I remember about a week before Lenya went to heaven, she and two-year-old Daisy were sitting opposite each other at this table. They were fighting and pushing it against each other. I told them to stop and to tell each other one thing they loved about the other.

Lenya immediately said, "I love Daisy's hair!"

Daisy quipped, "Well, I love her hair!" (Funny—for a long time, when we would ask Daisy something she loved about Lenya, her answer was always *her hair*.)

So I learned to embrace the table. But as I was writing this book, we had no choice but to get rid of it. It was falling apart, and all the chairs but one had broken after being fixed and screwed together multiple times. As wrecked as it was, I treasured this table even more because it reminded me of Lenya. It was difficult to get rid of something that had so many Lenya memories attached to it, such as the artwork she painted on the scratched-up wood, but I knew it had to go.

Levi and I gathered the kids together, and in Marie Kondo–like fashion, we talked about the fun and wild memories associated with the table. We were thankful for it and sad to say goodbye, but we knew it was time. There's no perfect way to get rid of sentimental items, if at all, but when you do, it's okay. Make a moment out of it. Weep if you've got to weep. Talk about the good memories, the difficulty of letting go. Thank God for His goodness. Walk through that painful moment and watch Him meet you there.

We now have a new addition in our home: a little white round table with little gold metallic chairs. It's a hip version of a kid's table that I still trip over, still curse about under my breath, and still have to fight in my heart to embrace. Yet I'm excited about all the new memories the children are creating around this one.

Enjoy the Process

Some seasons are really hard and seem like they're never going to end. When the kids were young, I remember feeling like all I did was change diapers. Granted, the feeling was legit because I *was* always changing diapers (and as of the writing of this chapter, I still am for baby number five!), but feeling like I couldn't see the end of it started to weigh me down. Once, I walked into a public restroom and saw a sign on the diaper changing station that read "This is only temporary." Thank you to whoever decided to post that sign! It was a perfect reminder that that time of my life was not going to last forever, and to enjoy it.

Levi and I have a special relationship with pastor Greg Laurie and his wife, Cathe, who lead Harvest Christian Fellowship. One reason we're so close is that we both have a child in heaven. They had visited us in Montana just three weeks before their thirty-three-year-old son died in a tragic car accident in July 2008. At that time, Lenya had just come home from being hospitalized due to her failure to thrive. It was the last time we would have with the Lauries and all of our kids. When Christopher arrived in heaven, Levi flew down to be with his family and speak at his funeral. When it was Lenya's turn, Greg came up to speak at her memorial service and the burial.

Cathe once told me about a moment she shared with Greg. At the time they had been married for forty years and had five grand-children. They were taking a walk with their grandkids, pushing two of them in a stroller, when she turned to her husband and said, "This is such a beautiful season!"

I've never forgotten that. I think of the day when Levi and I are older and wiser, walking with our grandkids all around us and enjoying them. Keeping that perspective in mind each day reminds us to immerse ourselves in the season we're in right now, so we can enjoy the season we will be in then.

If you're in a season that feels insignificant or especially long, look up. Set your gaze on who Jesus is. Ask God to help you see this season differently. Remember, you're already living from the finish line, but you're still in the middle of the process right now. This time in your life is part of the soil that is enriching your life and your future. Be here now.

When we engage in the daily fight and embrace the present moment, we will flourish. It's the little wins that change the course of our lives. We can live and love in the small moments of our everyday lives, knowing that there's an eternal significance to whatever God has called us to. So, when you're feeding your baby in the middle of the night and feeling run down by sleep deprivation, take a mental Instagram photo of that moment. Your baby is not going to eat like that at night forever. Or, if you're tired of being single and want to find your soulmate, remember you won't always have the kind of time you do currently. Savor where you are right now.

I am so thankful that in the few years leading up to Lenya's

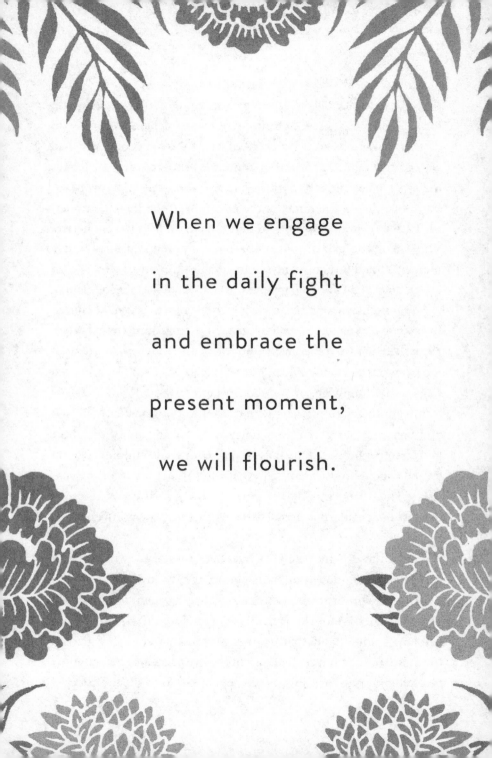

When we engage

in the daily fight

and embrace the

present moment,

we will flourish.

death, I was learning what it meant to enjoy the process. As imperfect as my journey was, I was aware of and saw the need to fight for this mind-set. I can't pin it down to one person telling me to do this; it was a beautiful cocktail of wisdom from people who had walked through it, of being in church leaning into my husband's messages, of learning the hard way, and of God speaking to my heart.

I love that in the midst of the craziness of the week Lenya left us, I have mental snapshots of her, memories I'll always cherish. They weren't necessarily out-of-the-ordinary events; just day-to-day moments that I immersed myself in and now treasure. I wrote down one of them right after it happened, and it still makes the kids laugh.

Two nights before Lenya went to heaven, we arrived at church from her ballet recital. She was wearing her leotard and tights. When we parked, Lenya immediately unbuckled and shot up toward me at the front of the Honda Pilot. "Mom!" she exclaimed. "I really need to go potty! Raindrops are falling through my body!"

In another memory, I remember Alivia taking a video of herself and Lenya in our greenroom. They were talking about root beer and champagne and "kids these days." Lenya was jumping around on the couches (not listening to the sitter) in her Snow White costume. Then there was the tea party with the girls on Wednesday because our regularly scheduled Tea Party Tuesday couldn't happen that week.

I love these memories. They have been tucked away in my heart for years and are now written in a book. What a joy!

If I had a do-over with Lenya the night she sought my attention, I would grab that moment with all my heart. I would tell her it would be okay. I would tenderly carry her upstairs. I would snuggle her, touch her beautiful face, look her in the eyes, listen to her, comfort her, and pray with her. I would lie next to her until she fell asleep.

I'm full of tearful regret and heartache when I realize I'll never get a second chance or that moment back. But I do see that I get the opportunity each day to walk in the little moments God has for me now. I know I won't always get it right, but I sure want to try.

9

God, Please Send Someone Else

Getting ready for church, or getting out of the house for anything first thing in the morning, is always chaotic. Wrangling four kids awake and making sure they're dressed appropriately (i.e., no flip-flops or leotards in winter, children!), fed, and out the door on time might as well be an Olympic event. Even if I plan the night before, it's still a madhouse in the morning.

This day, the weekend before Father's Day, we had to get to church to film a message for the following Sunday when Levi would be away. I barely had time to get myself dressed. I whipped out my favorite black motorcycle jeans that have the right amount of stretch and a black jacket with a silver tiger on the back. Black is easy; can't really mess it up. I pulled my hair up in a messy bun, grabbed the kids, and shuttled them into the car.

As we drove, I started to question what I was wearing. It didn't make me feel great. You know those days when you feel amazing because you nailed your outfit, and you're comfortable and confident and ready to conquer the world? I felt the opposite of that. My jacket was a little on the shorter side and my pants weren't high-rise (meaning, highly forgiving of a tummy that has carried five kids and thus accumulated extra skin). The black shirt underneath my jacket hid my muffin top, but still I didn't feel comfortable or confident.

Oh well, I shrugged. *It's not even a weekend service, so it's not like anyone's going to notice.* But I couldn't fake my way out of my feelings. My insecurity started to slowly inflate.

You see, Levi has a habit of asking me at the very last minute to get up on stage with him and encourage the church or share in our staff meetings. But in order to do this kind of thing, I tend to need to feel ready first. And that day I definitely did not feel ready.

Oh gosh, I hope Levi doesn't ask me to get on stage. My hair is a mess. My outfit's all wrong. Please, Lord. Not today!

Without even looking up from his phone, my husband said, "I think I'm going to bring you up on stage and have you do the introduction with me." He was telling me rather than asking me.

"Sure!" I replied with a smile. "That's a great idea."

Uh, no this is definitely not a great idea. I don't even have makeup on! My enthusiastic grin hid well my internal fight to not freak out.

As I was trying to talk myself off the ledge, Levi piped up again. "Give a little encouragement to the dads. Aaaaaand, I think it would be awesome if you wear Hulk hands."

The weekend was about honoring fathers as superheroes. We were planning on passing out water bottles with superhero labels slapped on them and having a photo booth where dads could take pictures with their kids wearing superhero props like capes and masks. So it made sense (obviously) for me to introduce the message with my hands fitted in gigantic, green Incredible Hulk fists.

I held on to my smile. "Okay, I can do that."

No, I can't do that. What the heck? This is so weird.

Second Timothy 4:2 came to mind: "Preach the word! Be ready

in season and out of season." Agreeing to Levi's plan was a small way of living out this verse. I couldn't help but laugh on the inside. I didn't feel ready mentally, having barely made it out of the house. I didn't feel ready physically, without makeup and with my hair in a messy-messy (not cool-messy) bun. (By the way, how do some girls have messy model hair that looks amazing no matter what, while I'm blessed with frizzy hair that makes me feel like I'm in sixth-grade basketball practice?) This was such a lesson for me to be ready to encourage and ready to give, whenever and wherever.

It wasn't about my hair or my outfit; the point was that I had something to share. And while I don't recommend rolling out of bed and immediately hopping on a platform to speak in front of a crowd without at least brushing your hair, giving others hope is what mattered most.

That morning, I had actually read Isaiah 38:19: "The living, the living man, he shall praise You, as I do this day; the father shall make known Your truth to the children." Wow, how perfect is that? And later, sporting those giant green hands, I was able to encourage the men in our church to teach their children how faithful God is.

We need to be ready for each opportunity God brings our way to encourage someone, to speak life into others, or to engage in a moment. God has uniquely designed us to love the people around us right where we are, right where they are. God loves the people in your life so much He put you in their lives. Let's be women who are ready!

You've Got What It Takes

I feel like an impostor sometimes, as if I'm living a life better suited to someone else. Me, married to one of the smartest and strongest and most patient husbands/preachers/storytellers of our time? Me, leading a stellar team that heads a trailblazing church in Montana, Oregon, Utah, Wyoming, and beyond? Me, travel the world with young children in tow? Me, preach the Word?

Doubt even creeps in as I write. Me, write a book? Shouldn't I do that when I'm old and gray and have way more wisdom and time than I do now? Who am I to teach when I struggle so much? Surely, someone else would do a better job. I have even found myself recently telling God, *I don't know if I can handle this responsibility. This weight seems too heavy for me. I think I might break. God, You should send someone else because I can't do this.*

There's a man in the Bible who said these same things. When God told Moses to lead the people of Israel out of Egyptian slavery, He promised Moses that He would be with him and help him. It's a really huge deal when the God who created the universe speaks to you and says that He's got your back. But instead of accepting the task with eagerness and gratitude, Moses hesitated. He began to list a litany of excuses, starting with, "Who am I that I should do this?" (Exodus 3:11, my paraphrase).

God wasn't upset by Moses' reluctance. In fact, He responded by encouraging the guy. "Don't worry, Moses. I'm going to be with you. Everything is going to work out just fine. You got this because *I've* got this!" (v. 12, my paraphrase). Boom, done!

Well, not quite. Moses kept backpedaling, "But what if nobody believes me?" (Exodus 4:1, my paraphrase).

To counter that, God performed miraculous feats to show Moses that He could do impossible things. I feel like that should have been the moment that Moses responded, "Wow, God! Okay, I'm in. Now I really know you've totally got this!"

But Moses still wasn't convinced. "Excuse me, God, Your miracles were mind-blowing, but the thing is, I'm not a good speaker. Like, I s-s-stutter. I'm a blubbering idiot. Trust me, no one is going to want to listen to me. *I* don't even like to listen to me!" (v. 10, my paraphrase).

God is so patient. He kept ignoring Moses' insecurity.

"Don't worry about it, Moses," God said reassuringly. "I'm going to speak through you. Just trust Me, okay? I know you are the right man for the job" (v. 12, my paraphrase). Moses, you got this!

I'd like to think if I were Moses, as unqualified as I feel at times, I'd give in at this point and say, "Okay, fine, God. I get it. I'm in!" But then again, who knows? After all, leading a nation of roughly two million people out of slavery isn't the easiest thing in the world to do. It's a massive assignment.

Moses looked up at God and sighed. Then, nervously kicking the dust with his worn-out sandal, he said, "Sorry, God. You'll just need to send someone else" (v. 13, my paraphrase).

This was where Moses went wrong and where God got mad. The Bible says His anger burned against Moses. Cringe. Bible commentator and our friend Pastor David Guzik makes a great point about this exchange:

God was not angry when Moses asked, "Who am I?" (Exodus 3:11). God was angry when Moses was just plain unwilling. There may be a hundred understandable reasons why Moses was unwilling, some of them making a lot of sense. Nevertheless, the basic truth was that Moses was unwilling, not unable.

What a sobering picture.

God can work with our insecurity. He can handle our weakness and feelings of inadequacy. But He can't work with someone who is unwilling to trust and obey Him.

Isn't Moses' reaction so relatable? How often do we find ourselves wanting to run in the opposite direction or hide in bed, under the covers? The idea that unwillingness is actually disobedience is a game changer for me. Whether or not I feel worthy or qualified or able, I want to say yes to God. I want to be in such a place of trusting Him that I am willing to do what He has asked me to do, whether it makes sense to me or not.

I pray that we would always have willing hearts. If God's got a job for us, He is going to give us the strength to do it, even if we feel we can't get it done.

On Father's Day this past year, my husband preached a message about courage and strength that changed me. Although Levi was primarily addressing men, God was speaking directly to me. The message focused on how Joshua stepped up and took Moses' place after Moses' death. God told Joshua, "As I was with Moses, so I will be with you. I will not leave you nor forsake you. Be strong and of good courage " (Joshua 1:5–6).

Levi's fourth point—*you've got what it takes*—is what got me. Levi pointed out that God told Joshua to *be* strong and courageous, not *feel* strong and courageous. This is a game changer. We often don't feel strong or worthy or qualified, so we sit back and wait for those feelings to come before we step out in faith and obey God. But God doesn't call us to feel strong; He calls us to be strong. Choose to be strong. Choose to walk in God's strength. Choose to be obedient. You've got what it takes. (Well, technically you don't. But you roll with a God who does.)

Go and Love Yourself

When we believe the lie that God should send someone else, it's probably because we're lacking in the self-love department. When we don't love ourselves, we stunt our growth.

Here's what I mean. The Bible commands us to love our neighbors as ourselves. But you can't do that well unless you pull a Justin Bieber—go and love yourself—first. And the best way to do that is to truly understand how much God loves you.

I like what Pastor Louie Giglio wrote in his relatable YouVersion reading plan:

> If you don't love yourself, you are actually negating the fact that God loves you. If you don't love yourself, it means you don't really understand God's perception of you—that you are an awesome, precious, one-of-a-kind treasure, valuable enough to warrant the pain and sacrifice of Jesus. . . .
>
> When the truth of God's love sinks into your heart, you can look in the mirror and say, "Well, if God sees me that way, then I'm going to see myself that way." When you do, you are acknowledging what God has already spoken from heaven about you.

When I read this, it stopped me in my tracks. What a life-changing perspective to say, "If God sees me as this treasure, then I'm going to choose to see myself that way." Remember, because we are in Christ—a new creation—when God looks at us, He sees Jesus.

Throughout my life I have struggled with how I see myself and had difficulty believing the best about myself.

I'm not the only one. Paul, who wrote much of the New Testament, talked about this inner struggle. In Romans 7, his frustration is evident when he described the tension between not doing what he should do and doing what he shouldn't do. He loved God and desired to serve Him, but at the same time, a part of him bucked against it. Read how exasperated he was: "O wretched man that I am! Who will deliver me from this body of death? I thank God—through Jesus Christ our Lord!" (vv. 24–25).

That word *wretched* means "miserable." Paul, an incredible leader, evangelist, author, and spiritual hero, admitted his struggle and called himself a wretched, miserable man! That's so intense. But I'm thankful for Paul's raw honesty, especially because more often than not I see myself through the same lens. Read my words for yourself:

May 25, 2013
156 days since I held Lenya last

Father, I'm so sorry for living most of my life with an improper attitude and conduct before You. I'm just so unknowing and I understand nothing and I hate looking back on my life and seeing what an idiot I've been. Focusing on things that don't matter, not focusing on the things that really do matter. Lord, I'm so disgusted with myself. But somehow, in it all, You love me deeply and I don't understand it, and I don't deserve it, but You freely give Your love and grace and peace and kindness and gentleness to me. So I respond to You with a heart of worship, from my little, weak heart to the heavens where Jesus is in His resurrected body, and where Lenya is in her perfect little pre-resurrected body. O Lord, may I live today in the light of that day. Oh to be like You.

I'm thankful Paul ended with "Who will deliver me from this body of death? I thank God—through Jesus Christ our Lord!" Boom! There's the answer: stick close to our Savior, who continually delivers us in our struggles to live as we were meant to live.

Stick close to
our Savior, who
continually
delivers us in
our struggles to
live as we were
meant to live.

I can't let my failures and faults stop me from clinging tightly to Jesus. I have to get back up. I have to learn from the past and let it launch me into the day and into the future. This keeps me from falling into the rabbit hole of negative self-talk, when I believe that I won't ever be good enough. Whenever I'm not living up to that picture on the seed packet, I say, "Jesus, Your grace is enough for me. Help me rest in You, enjoy You, and be confident in Your love."

Know That You're Loved

Since Lenya took her last breath on earth, one of the biggest things I've discovered is how deep God's love is for me. Yes, I know He loves the whole world . . . but *me*? Yes, me. I know I am loved by the One who created me and designed me beautifully with a unique and specific purpose for His glory. And He loves me especially when I experience great heartache.

The day after Lenya's death left the gaping, Lenya-shaped hole in our lives, Shayla, our lead songwriter and one of our worship leaders at Fresh Life, sent us a song she wrote called "Loved." She had finished writing it that morning, not knowing that our daughter had died the night before. When Shayla heard the news, heartbroken with us, she felt she should record the song and send it to us. Not knowing if it would be helpful, she was nervous to give it to us, but I'm glad she did. It became a buoy for our souls.

I remember listening to the song right away. We were hungry for any words, spoken or written—or in this case, sung—that God might speak over our aching hearts. I wept as I heard Shayla's beautiful voice sing lyrics that shook me to the core.

It's gonna be all right
It's gonna be okay
It's a cold dark night
But we'll find the day
Know that you're loved
Know that you're loved
And when the world starts to blur
And your soul gets heavy
And when you're at your worst
And the ground is unsteady
Know that you're loved
Know that you're loved
No matter what may come your way
You don't have to be afraid
No matter what you're fighting through
He'll be there holding you
No matter the sorrow, no matter how tough
Today and tomorrow, know that you're loved.

I know the song was special for Levi and for all who heard it with us, but I couldn't help but feel as though it were only for me. I tangibly felt God's love for me. It was as if the whole room blacked out and the spotlight from heaven—from God, my Lord, my Father, my Friend, who speaks His love and His peace over me—was shining only on me. Just as He had that night in New York City, God spoke to me through a faithful vessel.

This song became an anthem for our family. We chose to have Shayla sing it publicly for the first time at Lenya's celebration of life. It now sits cozy as the last song on our *Fall Afresh* album by Fresh Life Worship.

Don't strive

in your own

strength;

surrender to

the Spirit and

His strength.

I recently asked Shayla about the story behind the song. She wrote it for family friends who had just lost their seven-month-old son. Unable to wrap her head around such grief, Shayla decided to sing about the things she did know: that God holds and loves us right where we are, especially in the very worst thing we've ever faced.

Maybe you're like me and you have to fight to remind yourself that God loves you. That's okay; keep doing it. Keep yourself in the love of God. As it says in Jude: "But you, beloved, building yourselves up on your most holy faith, praying in the Holy Spirit, keep yourselves in the love of God, looking for the mercy of our Lord Jesus Christ unto eternal life" (Jude vv. 20–21).

Religion says, "Do this and then be." A relationship with Jesus says, "Be in Christ and then do." God's love isn't based on you; it's placed on you. You can rest in His love for you and then live, work, lead, and love from that place. Don't strive in your own strength; surrender to the Spirit and His strength.

In my moments of doubt, I pray like the man who asked Jesus to heal his son: "Lord, I believe; help my unbelief!" (Mark 9:24). We can be confident in His love, even when we're fighting to believe it.

This Is Love

When you're tempted to ask (or highly suggest) God to send someone else in your place, remember that He has called you to this. More than that—He also sends Himself with you. He's not just sitting ringside; He's in the ring with you, in your corner, fighting for you. He doesn't just want you to know He loves you; He's there to do something about it.

I was recently in a boxing class where the instructor had us working the bags. As we threw hooks and jabs, he started yelling, "Cross!" over and over. While pivoting our back feet, we repeated cross punches for a few very long minutes.

This is a solid illustration of how to remember God's love for us. Whatever you're in, whatever you're doing, whatever you're facing, keep the cross on your mind. Remind yourself and others, "Cross!" In the pain: "Cross!" In the feelings of inadequacy: "Cross!" When you want to say, "No thank You, God. This assignment must be for someone else," instead say, "Cross!"

God showed His love for us by sending His Son, Jesus, with the endgame of Him enduring a horrible death on a cross. Jesus came from heaven, was born as a baby, lived a sinless life, died an excruciating death, and rose from the dead, conquering death and guilt and shame forever.

After Jesus rose from the dead, He commissioned His disciples with the responsibility to go and reach people: "All authority in heaven and on earth has been given to me. Therefore go and make disciples of all nations, baptizing them in the name of the Father and of the Son and of the Holy Spirit, and teaching them to obey everything I have commanded you. And surely I am with you always, to the very end of the age" (Matthew 28:18–20 NIV).

I am with you always. Let these words sink down deep in the soil of your heart. When you feel like you can't go further, try to take the next step or the next breath, knowing God is with you. He will give you what you need. He will be what you need. And with this heart and this perspective, I believe you'll not only *not* say, "God, send someone else," but as Isaiah did when God spoke to him, you will say, "Here am I! Send me" (6:8).

10

You Can't Hug a Porcupine

For some reason, God decided it was good for me to have horns.

I have these little tufts of hair on either side of my head that, when left to their own wildness, protrude like horns. I'm sure God meant them to look like a cute ram thing, but I see them more as Maleficent horns or devil horns. Depends on the day, I guess. I can't blame this anomaly on the loss of hair before, during, or after having babies or because my hair is changing as I get older, because I've always had them.

I was having one of those days where I felt like an ogre. I hadn't left the house yet, I was still in my sweats, and I was in an overall funk. I picked up my phone, but the screen didn't turn on like it normally does. So instead of seeing the photo of my husband, three daughters, and baby boy—an image that always brings me joy—I saw my reflection. Well, more like a shadowy reflection; all I could see was my head and two horns sticking out of it.

It was a punch to my gut. *Oh man. I look how I feel!* This did not help my situation, but it did make me laugh at myself. And it reminded me to turn myself around and choose to have a humble heart and not harsh horns.

In my marriage, I tend to put up walls and defenses when I feel hurt or insignificant or unheard. When I have trouble communicating how I feel, I shut my husband out and hold things in, only to later lash out from seemingly nowhere and say hurtful things. Instead, I should let Levi in and involve him in what I'm feeling. Because God continues to teach me and because I'm married to a man who helps me see more clearly, I can now admit that I am indeed (*gulp*) passive-aggressive. I hate this, but it's my go-to response.

When I act out in this way, Levi calls it being a porcupine. He has told me (kindly, mind you) that it's hard for him to love me as he's supposed to when I'm not huggable but prickly. It's not the nicest analogy, but it's a fair one. You can't hug a porcupine—unless you love pain and want to be stabbed by its thirty-thousand-plus quills.

In any relationship, vulnerability is the key to intimacy. If our goal is to grow in our relationships, then we must let humility lead the way. God has some strong thoughts about this. First Peter 5:5 says, "Clothe yourselves with humility toward one another, because, 'God opposes the proud but shows favor to the humble'" (NIV). I don't want God against me because I don't humble myself. Rick Warren wrote about this idea: "This is true humility: not thinking less of ourselves, but thinking of ourselves less." Humility is a mind-set that will change the trajectory and depth of your relationships.

My friend and counselor, Debra Fileta, wrote an incredible book called *Choosing Marriage*. She wrote, "Humility has the power to bring two people together in a way that not many other things can manage to do." She then talked about a study that showed that couples who perceived a higher level of humility in their partners also had a higher level of commitment, trust, and forgiveness in their relationship, and an overall increase in relationship satisfaction. If

Humility is a

mind-set that

will change the

trajectory and

depth of your

relationships.

our friends and significant others even perceive humility in us, the relationship will be deeper.

That's certainly what I want, yet my actions often go in the opposite direction. Which reminds me of a story.

Prickliness Doesn't Pay

Before Lenya went to heaven, the plan was to leave the day after Christmas for California. One of the girls' Christmas gifts was a trip to Disneyland, but instead of seeing Sleeping Beauty's castle and having breakfast with Mickey Mouse, we celebrated Lenya's life on earth and buried her in an icy grave.

We headed to California a week later. Along with going to Disneyland, we also planned to spend time with Greg and Cathe Laurie, and their kids and grandkids. So there we were, visiting the Golden State, though it felt like we were living in a black-and-white film. Our grief was fresh and raw.

For the most part, Levi and I were on the same page in our sorrow. When we weren't, we tried our best to be patient with the other's lows and highs. But the day we drove to the Lauries', patience wasn't anywhere near my radar, and Levi and I were on nowhere near the same page. It was like we were in two totally different books.

I remember being so irritable, on edge. I knew Lenya was in heaven, but that truth didn't cure the ache of missing her. I couldn't handle it. I kept imagining Lenya running around with Alivia at the beach, or holding her hand at Disneyland, or her telling me about her day in her precious, raspy voice. And I hated that, because I wanted her. I kept thinking about all the things I was missing out on now, and all the future things I would never get to see, like watching her grow up, graduate high school, get married, be a part of her sisters' weddings.

I felt as though I were on the Guardians of the Galaxy ride—having my heart and stomach thrown all over the place during its unexpected drops and surges, leaving me sitting there at the end not knowing whether to laugh or cry or be quiet. Grief has a way of jerking around your emotions in a way you can't articulate. The only way I can define it is "weird." There is no rhyme or reason or rhythm to grief.

As special as the whole Laurie family is to our family and to me personally, I just didn't want to be anywhere but home that day. Sitting in our car parked in their driveway, I turned to Levi. With my face showcasing my best porcupine scowl, I attempted a last-ditch effort to leave: "I'd just rather not be here right now."

Levi sighed. "Well, we're here. Let's just hang out." His tone was patient.

Not mine.

When we got out of the car to get Clover's stroller out of the trunk, I yelled at Levi. I'm not proud to admit it. The kids were still in the car, so they heard it. I then told him I needed a minute to take a walk around the block. A walk can change everything.

Before I set out, I said something to Levi. Well, it wasn't exactly *to* Levi; it was under my breath, and he wasn't supposed to hear it. (Here's some advice: if you have to say something under your breath, you probably shouldn't say it at all.) Anyway, I muttered a two-word directive for Levi to . . . do something. I know, not my finest moment as a wife.

I immediately regretted what I said. Now my anger was joined by a new friend named Shame.

I grabbed the stroller, strapped Clover in it, and began my walk fuming. I was angry. Mad that Lenya wasn't here. Mad at Levi. Mad that I was mad and I couldn't get ahold of myself. As I pushed the stroller down the block, tears streamed from my face. *God*, I prayed silently. *This is the worst Jennie I've ever been. I'm mad. I'm sad. I'm things I don't even know I am. I need You to help me be kind. I need You to help me be the loveable version of me You created me to be. I need Your strength.*

I started to settle down. The walk was helpful; I felt more peace than fury. By the time I found myself back at the car, I had calmed down. (And Levi had actually waited for me—true gentleman alert.) But it was one of those moments when we didn't have time to fully talk through what had happened and kiss and make up.

Levi and I ended up spending precious time with the Lauries. We were vulnerable and shared our heartache and our struggle. As good friends do, they spoke life and encouragement and love over us.

The day ended on a slightly traumatic note at an urgent care medical facility. Clover fell backward off the bottom step of their house, hit her head, and had the wind knocked out of her. Before our eyes, she turned pale and lethargic. As Levi and I sat with Clover in the hospital, bombarded with horrible flashbacks from two weeks earlier, I genuinely apologized to Levi, and we talked through the earlier tension. In that room, I was reminded that we are not fighting against each other but for each other, and we're in the other's corner.

Lesson learned: Prickliness doesn't pay.

Learning to Melt

Feeling mad isn't wrong. How I yelled and threw a tantrum, however, was. The Bible says to "Be angry, and do not sin" (Ephesians

4:26). I had to get a grip on myself. I had to come to a place of humility and vulnerability and repentance. I had to stop being a defensive porcupine, ready to raise my sharp quills and shoot them toward those who love me most.

Levi and I have a special word for when I take a step back, humble myself, and choose to see differently. We call it *melting*. Instead of keeping my fists clenched toward him when I'm upset, I'm learning to let my guard down and open up to him. Even if I can't articulate exactly what's going on, I'm vulnerable enough to let him in and say, "I'm hurting. This is hard for me. When you said or did _____, it really got to me." This gives my husband the space to respond. No one yells. No one says things they're going to regret.

I'll be the first one to admit that melting isn't easy, but I'll also say it's always worth it.

Proverbs 15:1 says: "A soft answer turns away wrath, but a harsh word stirs up anger." I've always thought this verse referred to the dynamic between two people: one person's softness soothes another's anger; one's sharpness triggers the other to respond in the same way. But I also think that it can describe the inner dynamic within a person: in other words, my own soft answer can turn away my own wrath, and my harsh word can stir up my own anger.

Speaking harshly generates anger in the other person, but it also does the same in my own heart. If I can let my heart melt, that softness can actually turn away the wrath in my own soul. I can fight for the gentle response that causes my anger to dissolve.

More than just punching anger in the gut with a soft answer, reacting in a harsh and angry way misrepresents God to the people in our lives. The Bible tells us that this is a big deal.

Remember Moses, who declined God's call and asked Him to send someone else in his place? He did eventually deliver the

Israelites out of slavery. Imagine the logistics of such a thing: one man with a few assistants, piloting about two million people through the middle of nowhere. There were no iPhones with GPS or Waze; Moses couldn't send a group text informing the Israelites, "Hey, everyone, we're packing up and leaving at 7:00 a.m. tomorrow. Don't forget your wives and goats and children. Sally, please keep track of your donkey this time. George, try to keep up."

Logistics aside, imagine listening to these people complain. Which they did. A lot. "We're thirsty!" "We're hungry!" "There's nothing to eat!" "Why did you even bring us here?"

On one particular day, God's people whined, "Moses! Did you lead us out here to die? You tricked us! There isn't any food or water! We hate you, Moses. You're the worst!" (Numbers 20:4–5, my paraphrase).

This would have made me so mad. I probably would have said, "Fine, guys. You win. I quit. You're on your own now. Good luck finding the promised land! See you in heaven someday."

Not Moses. Instead, he fell on his face before God and asked for help. God told Moses to speak to a rock and that water would come out. Simple enough.

But Moses didn't listen. Instead of talking to the rock, he hit it. But before he did, he turned to the people and lashed out in anger and bitterness. "You bunch of bleepity-bleep . . ." Okay, maybe he didn't use an expletive, but he was annoyed with them and called them rebellious (v. 10).

Now, hitting the rock instead of speaking to it doesn't seem like a big deal, but it really was. Moses didn't believe God, nor did he obey Him. He let his anger lead him, and that was wrong, even if the people were being whiny and unreasonable. When we are harsh and allow our emotions to lead the way, we misrepresent God. We don't portray a God of love.

Getting angry is not the problem. It's what we do with it that's most important. Will we allow God to soften our hearts so we can truly melt before the cross, or will we snap in disobedience and misrepresent God to those we lead? When we choose to melt, we're choosing to not miss out on the mission God has set before us. We choose a better way.

Let Others In

After Lenya went to heaven, there were times I felt alone. One of my strengths is empathy, but it can also be a weakness when it keeps me from reaching out to others when I'm in pain. I know everyone has so much going on, and I sincerely don't want to be a burden. Pride also keeps me from leaning on friends. It used to take so much courage to ask someone to pray for me or to ask for help. It felt unnatural, and I'd have much preferred to muscle through on my own.

When my defenses are up and I don't admit my need for others, two things happen: I rob myself of the wisdom someone can speak into my life, and I rob someone of the opportunity to give and be a friend.

A special exchange happens when we share our deepest feelings with others. Look at what the Bible says can happen: "Confess your sins to each other and pray for each other so that you may be healed" (James 5:16 NIV). True healing comes from vulnerability. We need each other more than we think we do.

The Enemy wants us to hide our hearts from others. He whispers in our ears anything he can use to keep us isolated and disconnected. *You're the only one struggling with this; other people won't understand and will judge you.* Or maybe, *If you tell her what you're really feeling,*

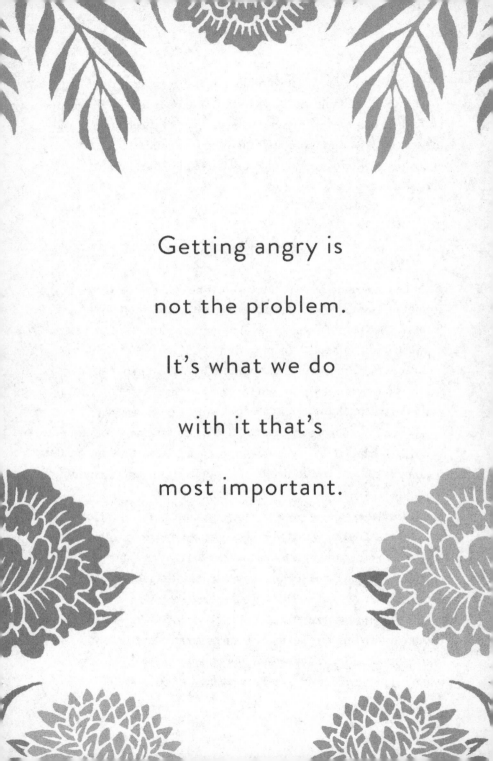

Getting angry is

not the problem.

It's what we do

with it that's

most important.

she'll never want to be your friend. God knows the power and healing that happens when we speak up, and so should we.

When we bring others into our pain, we position ourselves to receive wisdom, insight, and a different perspective that we wouldn't have gained otherwise. But finding and nurturing deep relationships takes time. They don't happen magically.

I was heading to the airport after attending Colour Conference 2018, and somehow the driver ended up telling me about the cat he'd adopted. He and his family already had one cat at home, so they had to strategically and very slowly integrate them. Apparently, having a new animal in the home can trigger territorial panic. He told me he first introduced them and then separated them. Gradually, he extended their time together until the two cats felt totally comfortable with each other. It was a long process; in fact, it often takes cats about a year to become friends.

When Levi and I moved from Albuquerque to Southern California a year after we got married, I was plunged into a new environment and a new church with new people *everywhere.* This new church family was welcoming and kind, but it took me about a year to find a few close friends. Honestly, I think it took too long. I'd like to say that, if I'd known then what I know now, I would have made the choice sooner to open up more and let people in.

God had us in California for less than two years. I wonder how much deeper my relationships would have been had I committed and invested in others a little more. I don't know, but I do know I want to be a better friendship former, not a friendship finder.

I just recently found out that there are porcupines that are actually huggable and, therefore, holdable when a friend told me that she had held a baby porcupine. A baby porcupine is called a porcupette, and they're born with soft quills and lots of fuzz so that their mothers can give birth to them. (That's an image for you: a porcupine giving birth.) But I think the posture of a porcupette is paramount in this conversation.

If in my porcupine moments I can pull a Transformer move and switch myself into porcupette mode—soft, playful, touchable, and cuddly—life will be so much better for me, and for all those who come in contact with me.

If we're truly going to flourish, we need to fight off what keeps us from growing and let in what causes us to thrive. Sadly, we often get in our own way; we let our horns stick out or we deploy our porcupine quills, and we scare away the very people we need and who need us. If instead we embrace porcupette qualities, we can let in those who are in our corner—an invaluable source of support as we grow into the vibrant, vigorous lives we are destined to live.

11

Stir Up the Sweetness

I have face problems. And it's not just when I try to unlock my phone in the morning and it tells me "Face not recognized. Try Face ID again." *Really, phone? You're going to treat me like that right when I wake up in the morning? I know my face isn't what it once was, but still. Not cool.*

What I mean is the following kind of face problem: A few years ago, Levi and I were talking, and I was bummed at something he had said. I didn't tell him, though. I just listened to him and did what comes naturally to me—processed his response internally.

Levi suddenly stopped talking, looked at me, and asked, "What's your face doing?"

"What do you mean?" I shot back. Who was I kidding? I knew exactly what he meant.

Some peoples' hips don't lie, but it's my face that doesn't. If I'm happy, you know it. If I'm mad, you know it. If I'm disappointed, you know it. Not only that, but whenever I'm deep in thought or reading, I catch myself frowning and making the lines (aka the elevens) on my forehead more pronounced. I look bummed, serious, even un-approachable. So the sign on my face is basically saying, "Go away!

Beware all ye who enter here!" Not only that, but my tone tends to match my facial expression. Both these things frustrate my husband and anyone else on the receiving end. It especially frustrates me, though, because I know I can do better and be sweeter.

My heart is to be at my best with my husband, my kids, and those closest to me, but at times I'm at my worst with them. The moment I speak with a snippy tone or have an ungrateful look, I know it. I feel it. I hate it. And I immediately regret it. Moments like these make me evaluate how I respond to people and why.

I can't control others or their responses, but I can control myself. I love how Lance Witt, author of *High Impact Teams*, puts it: "When it comes to your life, you hold the position of CLO: chief life officer. That doesn't mean you control everything in your world, but it does mean you are responsible for leading yourself." I am the CLO of my life—no one else's. As hard as it may feel in the moment, I can control my attitude, my facial expressions, the atmosphere of my heart.

I don't have to let my frustration turn into frostiness. Instead of immediately reacting to someone negatively, with critique or judgment, I want to be a woman who responds strongly with compassion, understanding, and sweetness. The Bible tells us to be quick to hear, slow to speak, and slow to anger (James 1:19). That's a fight for most of us. But as we lean into God, we can look up and, like the writer of Psalm 34:5 said, be like those who "looked to Him and were radiant, and their faces were not ashamed." #FaceGoals

Kind Eyes

Paul wrote, "Be kind to one another, tenderhearted, forgiving one another, even as God in Christ forgave you" (Ephesians 4:32). Some of us are naturally kind, tenderhearted, and forgiving. Others have to work harder at it. And that's okay, because we're learning and growing, and God is working on us.

I look at it this way: If God's kindness leads us to repentance (Romans 2:4), it means He looks at us with kind eyes. He doesn't respond to the ugly things we do or say with a frown, or with disappointment, or with blame. He looks at us with love in His eyes. If God can look at me this way, while I'm still in the midst of all my sin and flaws and failures, how can I not look at my husband, my children, and the people I encounter in the same way?

I'd say most of us women love making our eyes pretty. We apply shimmery eye shadow, mascara, eyeliner, and eyelash extensions to try to make our eyes sparkle. We also dab on eye creams to try to lessen the blow of the aging process. Now, I'm not an anti-makeup kind of girl and I think it's important to take care of the skin we're in, but no amount of glittery makeup or faux eyelashes can make our eyes kind. This happens on the inside. It's a heart issue. Kind eyes get their running start from the soul.

First Peter 3:4–5 says, "Cultivate inner beauty, the gentle, gracious kind that God delights in" (THE MESSAGE). Our inner beauty flows out of our eyes, our mouths, our hearts. Think about this: If it's true that the eyes are the window to the soul, are you stirring up a sweetness in your soul that shines through your eyes and glimmers through your life? If you're struggling to say yes, I've got a solution for you.

If we are to have kind eyes toward others, we need to first look to the One who looks at us this way. This is where sweetness begins. Before we made the decision to trust in Jesus, there was a hole in our hearts that only He could fill. We were lost and stuck in our sin with no way out on our own. God made the way by sending us a savior, His only Son, Jesus, to die for us, to rise up from the grave, and through this to bring us hope, freedom, and life. Forgiveness was our biggest need because sin was our biggest problem. If we can fully receive God's forgiveness, then forgiveness will flow from us, and from that well we will be kind and tenderhearted to those around us.

Sunflowers face the sun all day. How much kinder will our hearts and eyes be if we're looking to our Sun, our Creator and Savior, throughout the day? Let's embody Hebrews 12:2 by "looking unto Jesus, the author and finisher of our faith."

Warmth Is Key

Hebrews 10:24 gives us a great picture of what it means to stir up the sweetness: "And let us consider one another in order to stir up love and good works." A couple of things here. One, the word in Greek for "stir up" has an aggressive tone to it. It speaks of provocation. Some translations use the word *spur*. If you're a horse lover, you know that some riders wear metal spurs on their boots and use them to apply pressure to the horse in order to urge it forward. Part of stirring up the sweetness is allowing the right people in our lives to stir it up in us.

Two, a key to stirring up love and good works in each other is warmth. Warmth is "the quality of being intimate and attached; an effect of brightness, cheerfulness, coziness, etc., achieved by the use of warm colors." It's impossible to stir up the sweetness with a cold heart; you need warmth. And similarly, you also need warmth to make sweet tea.

I know it's a Southern thing and I'm from California, but sweet tea is my favorite. If I could choose any drink and didn't have to think about the sugar, calories, and other annoying worries, hands down it would be sweet tea—specifically, sweet tea from Chick-fil-A.

To make sweet tea, I boil water, add the tea bags, let them steep for a while, and then add a cup of sugar. This is a fun process to do with the girls because when I add the sugar and stir the mixture, the sugar dissolves and seems like it disappears. Homeschool science experiment and delicious treat all at once. The sugar isn't gone, of course; it's just stirred into the tea. Finally, add ice and enjoy my happy drink.

It's pretty much impossible to sweeten tea when it's cold. If you've ever tried this, you know what I mean. I've gone to restaurants and asked for sweet tea only to have the server tell me (usually with a judgmental tone), "I'm sorry. We don't do sweet tea, but we have sweeteners you can add to our iced tea." *Nooooo! It's so not the same thing!* It's just adding sugar to the bottom of cold tea, then drinking sugar through the bottom of a straw for the first few minutes until it goes back to regular tea. Sugar doesn't dissolve well in cold water. There's actually science behind it: Hot water has more energy than cold water. As the molecules in hot water move faster, they have more contact with the sugar, causing it to dissolve faster. Heat stirs the sweetness.

In the same way, warmth gathers people together. We gather around a bonfire, a meal, a living room with a fireplace, a pot of hot coffee or tea. As Hebrews 10:24 indicates, there's a warmth within us that stirs up the sweetness in people around us to spur us on toward love and good works. But this warmth in our own souls is something we also need to fight for. We can't do it in our own strength, only through the power of the Holy Spirit.

The Spirit empowers us to have a good attitude, to show love and not exclude, to extend grace and not ignore, to use words that encourage and do not tear down, to smile and not frown (I'm preaching to myself here). In our homes, in our workplaces, and in our communities, we are called to create space for people to feel welcomed, invited, and loved—the way we can help those around us flourish.

Smile and Wave

Stirring up the sweetness is a lifestyle of kindness, in big and small ways. Recently I was about to turn right out of a parking lot onto the main road. A woman driving in the lane I was trying to squeeze into looked like she was going to let me in. As I started to merge into the flow of traffic in front of her, I smiled and gave her a "You're-going-to-let-me-in, right?" look, to which she promptly responded by shaking her head. "Oh no," her face said. "I am definitely not going to let you in." Guess I was totally off. But too late: I sneaked in front of her and didn't even look back to see how mad it made her.

Maybe I shouldn't have forced my way in, but how much easier would it have been for her to create a space for me to pull in front of her? How much energy would it have taken for her to just smile back, nod, and wave me in? I mean, really!

One thing I say a lot is, "Just smile and wave." I actually quote the head penguin, Skipper, from the movie *Madagascar*: "Just smile and wave, boys. Smile and wave." Yes, it's a funny quote that my kids laugh at almost every time, but there's also some truth in there.

A smile can leave a huge mark in this world. For the record: yes, I often do smile and wave to people, even ones I don't know. In fact, there are many times when I wave to someone when Levi and I are driving around town, and he asks, "Who was that?" I often respond by raising my shoulders and eyebrows saying, "I have no

We are called to

create space for

people to feel

welcomed, invited,

and loved—the way

we can help those

around us flourish.

idea." Sometimes it's someone I know; sometimes it's not. In a small town, we're probably passing by someone we know, so technically I can't go wrong smiling and waving at everyone.

(The instructor in my self-defense class said that while it's important to carry yourself in a confident way, you don't need to smile at everyone. When I heard that, my smile-and-wave bubble burst a little. But she's right; we should always be aware of our surroundings and act accordingly.)

My point here is that we can have a smile-and-wave spirit and show it to the world. We can show kindness to the people we come across every day, whether we know them or not. Let's continue to fight for what Paul commanded us to do: "Imitate God, therefore, in everything you do, because you are his dear children" (Ephesians 5:1 NLT). See people. Be kind. Ask them how they are and really care about what they have to say. Pray for others. Practice self-control. In your car or down the hall, morph your pouty face into a sweet smile and, while you're at it, wave. You never know how such a simple gesture can make a lasting impact.

Sugar Lips

One of the obvious ways we can stir up the sweetness is with our words. I love the beauty of these ancient words of wisdom:

> The lips of the wise give good advice;
> > the heart of a fool has none to give. (Proverbs 15:7 NLT)

> The king is pleased with words from righteous lips;
> > he loves those who speak honestly. (Proverbs 16:13 NLT)

The Lord detests evil plans,
>   but he delights in pure words. (Proverbs 15:26 NLT)

A soft answer turns away wrath,
>   But a harsh word stirs up anger. (Proverbs 15:1)

What's on your lips? I'm not talking about your shimmery lip gloss, or your brick-red lipstick, or your sugary-tasting Chapstick with SPF 30. I'm talking about the words that come out of your mouth. Do you speak truth or what you think someone wants to hear? Do you respond with a soft answer or harsh words? Does love flow from your soul through your lips to the people who need life spoken over them?

Jesus said, "Out of the abundance of the heart his mouth speaks" (Luke 6:45). What's in your heart will come out of your mouth. I'm not saying every conversation needs to be super-spiritual and intense, but the sweet tone of your soul should steadily spill out onto others.

"Death and life are in the power of the tongue" (Proverbs 18:21), so think before you respond. Speak thankfulness. Speak honor. Speak encouragement. Have more good things to say than negative. Use your words to bring life to others, not verbally knock them out.

What about the words we don't speak but type? It's so easy to complain, point fingers, judge, and whine online. Being transparent is a good thing, but it's equally important to use our words well on the internet. If the world will know that we love God by our love for each other, that includes what we say to or about others on our social media platforms. I've read posts and comments that break my heart. I get mad when I see people who say they love Jesus use their

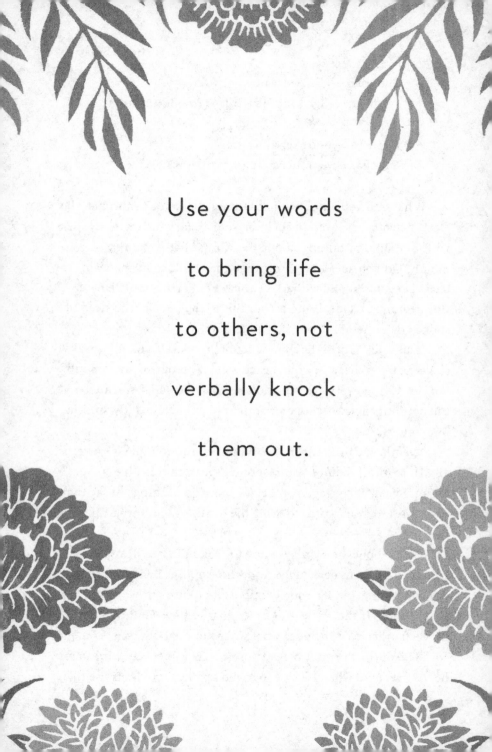

Use your words

to bring life

to others, not

verbally knock

them out.

words to bash others. It's ugly. I have a bitter taste in my mouth just thinking about it.

It's been said that those of us who follow Jesus should be known more for what we are for than what we are against. Let's be known for the real love we have in Jesus—and use our spoken and written words just so.

Winsome Living

I love the word *winsome*, which means "sweetly or innocently charming; winning; engaging." How lovely is this? It reminds me of another proverb (if you couldn't tell by now, the book of Proverbs in the Bible is a great resource for wise and winsome living): "The fruit of the righteous is a tree of life, and he who wins souls is wise" (11:30). This is true winning, true winsomeness, a picture of the sweetness of the soul pouring out into a world in desperate need of a touch from God.

Second Corinthians 2:15 says, "For we are to God the fragrance of Christ among those who are being saved and among those who are perishing." We are meant to be God's perfume (a good one!) to a hurting world. We don't gather in church to belong to a club. We are meant to scatter and be lights in the world. We are the welcome mat to Jesus to those who don't know Him. We are light to those who are in darkness.

When we sweeten our words with hope and joy and kindness, God can use us to reach someone at the gym, in the office, on an airplane, or in our own family. We react and respond to others with purpose. Through our words and winsomeness, we can create room at the table for people to come, taste, and see that the Lord is good (Psalm 34:8). That's what I want to fight for.

Put on Love

Jesus was winsome. The way He interacted with people helped them understand how He wanted them to live—and some of His instructions were tough pills to swallow. Like this one:

> "You have heard that it was said, 'You shall love your neighbor and hate your enemy.' But I say to you, love your enemies, bless those who curse you, do good to those who hate you, and pray for those who spitefully use you and persecute you, that you may be sons of your Father in heaven; for He makes His sun rise on the evil and on the good, and sends rain on the just and on the unjust." (Matthew 5:43–45)

Oh, man. I'm feeling the sting of conviction right now. Pray for those who use you and persecute you? Do good to the haters? These are really hard messages for me. And they are definitely not the first things that jump to my mind when people are being mean to me, or more so, mean or critical of my husband or the people I love.

My first reaction is to do what King David did: pray for God to punch my enemies in the face and shatter their teeth. Seriously, David prayed this one time. His fantasy was for God to knock his enemies' teeth out (Psalm 58:6)—and sometimes that's mine too. I know, it's the opposite of winsome. And it's not terrible to initially feel this way. God can handle our honesty, but He doesn't want us to stay there. I've learned to move from wanting to give a hurtful person a good uppercut, to *not* wanting to do that, to asking God to help me love them, to then asking Him to bless them. (And usually the space between those last two is wide.) More importantly, I ask Him to help me do what I can't do on my own.

Levi and I were recently browsing in a department store in Chicago. As I looked around the women's clothing section, he texted me to meet him in skincare. When I found him, he was holding a bottle of perfume. "You like this brand, right?" he asked with excitement.

I did. It was my favorite: a juniper scent. It smelled incredible; subtle, not flowery. Levi calls me Juniper, so when I first discovered this perfume, it was love at first smell. And I had just run out of it. With a big grin, Levi told me, "Pick your new scent."

After sniffing a few fragrances, I chose one called Elevator Music. The idea behind it was to create a perfume that was super subtle and that stayed in the background, like elevator music. It won the prize in my olfactory contest.

The person who rang up my purchase asked if I'd like to monogram my new bottle. I never knew that was a thing. My immediate response was, "Yes, please. 'Put on Love.'" I wanted to be reminded that just as I have the choice to put on something that makes me smell wonderful, I also have the choice to put on love.

Colossians 3:12–14 says, "Therefore, as God's chosen people, holy and dearly loved, clothe yourselves with compassion, kindness, humility, gentleness and patience. Bear with each other and forgive one another if any of you has a grievance against someone. Forgive as the Lord forgave you. And over all these virtues put on love, which binds them all together in perfect unity" (NIV).

Most of us put thought into the clothes we wear. *Should I dress up today? Maybe just jeans. My workout tights could work too. Sweatpants it is.* How much more should we consider with care the compassion, humility, and patience that we put on?

I love that after Paul taught us how to live, he told us to put on love. Love is like the glue that holds everything together; it creates a perfect unity. Wow! I need that.

Put on love—and put it on every day.

Maybe you don't like perfume but use essential oils. My friend uses an oil called Joy every day. It smells wonderful, but she says it's also the act of putting it on that helps her mind-set. Choosing to put on joy? Game changer. There is power in the application.

It's not easy to be sweet or gentle or loving when we're feeling pain. Yet it's possible not to allow that pain to turn us into ogres. Rather, we ought to strive to be women who love people and who love to bless people.

Here is one of the scriptures I lean toward when I'm dealing with my response to tough situations:

Summing up: Be agreeable, be sympathetic, be loving, be compassionate, be humble. That goes for all of you, no exceptions. No retaliation. No sharp-tongued sarcasm. Instead, bless—that's your job, to bless. You'll be a blessing and also get a blessing. (1 Peter 3:8–12 THE MESSAGE)

The message is clear: our job is to bless others, to be agreeable, sympathetic, loving, compassionate, humble. In the New King James Version, the same passage uses words like "be of one mind," "tenderhearted," and "courteous."

People are messy. Some are hard to deal with. But we can still bless them. When we're offended, bless. When we've been betrayed, bless. When we're afraid, bless. When we're having a bad day, bless. When we do this, we can say, without any sarcasm attached, "Bless their heart."

It's going to be a fight to stir up the sweetness in your soul. In my experience, it's a daily one. To be the pleasant and tenderhearted person you were created to be requires remembering how God views you, cultivating your relationship with Jesus, and humbling yourself before God and others. When we live like this, what springs out of our lives will cause others to see the Source of our sweetness, and they will be inspired to stir it up in their own souls.

12

Stronger Together

Tossing and turning, I felt angst swelling in my heart. As cozy as the fluffy pillow felt under my head, heaviness weighed me down. And it wasn't the good kind of heaviness, like a weighted blanket that makes you surrender to sleep under its comforting bulk.

Levi was asleep next to me, snoring. The more I heard his deep, relaxed breathing in the silence of midnight, the more annoyed I got. *He has no idea I'm struggling, and he doesn't care.* Feeling very alone, my frustration morphed to sadness. I got out of bed and began to weep.

Psalm 73 immediately came to mind.

> Whom have I in heaven but You?
> And there is none upon earth that I desire besides You.
> My flesh and my heart fail;
> But God is the strength of my heart and my portion forever.
> (vv. 25–26)

Then, it hit me. Well, really, God hit me (gently) with questions: *Am I all you need? Do you want anyone else on earth besides Me?* The more I thought about it, the more I realized I hadn't been keeping Jesus where He belonged in my heart—front and center. I had put Levi there instead, and that was an unfair thing for me to do to my husband.

Though that night was the first time I truly understood how much I had depended on Levi, I'd dealt before with the effects of my reliance on him blowing up. Before we knew Lenya was suffering from failure to thrive, and countless doctor appointments and tests pointed to nothing, I wrote in my journal:

This has been a hard year and then to add all the medical bills on top of that—OVERWHELMING and I feel like I'm drowning. But, Lord God, You know. You know my heart, my mind, my worries, anxieties, frustrations—You have searched me and known me. I cry out to You. I need You because I haven't clung to You like I should and therefore I've been unrealistically and unfairly expecting from Levi.

It's hard not to expect support from Levi because he's strong and smart and consistent and loves Jesus and wears these rose-colored glasses through which he views life. But still, Levi is Levi. And God is God.

Levi was sleeping because he's human and humans need sleep. God wasn't sleeping because He is God and the Bible says He never slumbers or sleeps (Psalm 121:4). Not only does my Father in heaven not sleep, but He's also near to me. And more than that, He knows me better than I know myself. He knows the deepest parts of me.

In that moment, God knew my struggle. He was the one I needed to cry out to and run to. But I was also able to share my concerns with Levi the next morning, get his perspective, and ask him to pray for me.

I can't expect my

human relationships

to be what only

my relationship

with God can be.

That night was a turning point for me. I can't expect my human relationships to be what only my relationship with God can be. And yet, I need the human relationships that God has given me.

There's a beautiful tension here: God is all we need, yet we're better and stronger because of the people He has put in our lives. We just can't let them take the place only reserved for the King.

All aboard the Friend-Ship

Looking through the lens of hindsight, I see that God has placed people in my life for specific reasons or in certain seasons. This has shown me how much I need them and how much they need me.

An important part of the fight to flourish is who we do life with. I've heard it stated that a typical friendship lasts about three to five years. I was shocked when I heard this. I can count on one hand the number of friends I still somewhat connect with from high school. And friends from elementary school? Just a few fingers. While I know that lifelong friends are a rarity, I guess I figured once you had a friend, you'd always be friends.

If we're believers, we're family, so in a way we're stuck together. We'll be hanging out forever in heaven, right? Part of me assumed if I'm friends with you now, we'll always be friends. But I have found that's not always the case. Some friendships fade naturally. Some grow stronger through the distance. The friendships we thought we'd have for life end early for myriad reasons. And then sometimes we're surprised by friends who enter our lives seemingly randomly but stick with us through thick and thin.

Healthy friendships can't be controlled or even figured out. True friendships are a gift from God no matter how long they last.

It's important to have a light touch when it comes to friendships—to be willing to both receive new friends and let go of old ones. Understanding this radically changed my perspective on friendship. I learned I can be a blessing to friends as they come and as they go. Isn't that the point—to have an impact on the people in our lives? However long your friendships last, you can embrace them, enjoying the ones you have in the moment. You can receive strength and wisdom from them, and be a strong and wise and kind friend in return.

All of this talk about friendship reminds me of one of my favorite women in the Bible: Ruth. I like to imagine that she and I would get along really well. I can't wait to spend time with Ruth in heaven. (Sometimes, I wonder how meeting people in heaven works. Will there be a really long line for some people, like the OGs in the Bible, and no line for others—like at Disneyland, where the line for Mickey Mouse is a mile long but an obscure character from *Pinocchio* is wandering around alone? Welcome to my random thought life.)

Ruth's name actually means "friendship." She was loyal, trustworthy, committed, and determined; she honored the authority in her life and was just all-around pleasant. Ruth was the kind of friend you want to have and the kind of friend you want to be. I like to think that she models for us how to be the kind of friend we were born to be. That she shows off the fashion of friendship and what it looks like to just be there for someone.

There for You

What if this overarching statement could be said about us as women?
We're there for each other.
I believe this is the kind of friend we were born to be. God

created us for friendship, to engage in deep, meaningful relationships where we're aware of each other's pain, share our struggles, and engage with transparency. Not just the surface stuff.

This is where Ruth's example helps me so much. I could read her whole story every day. It's only four chapters long, so it's totally doable in one sitting. (I wish I could just include it right here, but I'd exceed my word count.) Let me encourage you to read it for yourself.

In the beginning of her story, we discover Ruth living in a city called Moab with her husband and in-laws. Ten years later, her husband, brother-in-law, and father-in-law died. Naomi, Ruth's mother-in-law, decided to return to her hometown, and Ruth joined her. They didn't really have a plan or a support network, which was important for a widow. Ruth chose to follow Naomi knowing full well that she would be the one taking care of Naomi. *That* is a good friend.

Ruth's declaration of her commitment to be there for Naomi is beautiful to me:

> "Entreat me not to leave you,
> Or to turn back from following after you;
> For wherever you go, I will go;
> And wherever you lodge, I will lodge;
> Your people shall be my people,
> And your God, my God.
> Where you die, I will die,
> And there I will be buried.
> The LORD do so to me, and more also,
> If anything but death parts you and me." (1:16–17)

She's saying, "We are family, and there's no way you're getting rid of me, because I'm here, and I'm here to stay."

Ruth got a job to provide for her mother-in-law. Later, she is described as being better to Naomi than seven sons (4:15). She was there for her new mother.

What does it look like to be there for someone who is suffering? How do you walk with a friend through their pain? It can be so hard to know what to do, what to say, how to act, whether or not to be there. Let me encourage you to be there, to be sensitive to the Holy Spirit leading you. What helped me when Lenya went to heaven was when people came in with a meal or to help with my kids. The friends who were there, who sat with me, who didn't say anything profound, who told me they were praying for me—that made an impact on my grieving heart.

My friend Holly Furtick, who so graciously wrote the foreword for this book, was that kind of friend. But she didn't know me. She felt the push to reach out to me. On December 24, 2012, four days after Lenya died, Holly texted me to introduce herself, and in her text she included, "My heart hurts for you guys right now. I don't have any words of wisdom and comfort for you but I would like to text you scriptures that may bring encouragement here and there. I am praying for you and would love to help you in any way . . ."

For the next three years, Holly sent random texts to me, sharing God's Word and encouraging me by saying she was praying for me and thinking of me. It's a rare person who will be so consistent, but I'm thankful for how she was there for me, even through texting from far away. I'm not saying you should do exactly what she did for each of your friends; that wouldn't be possible. But I am saying that you can ask God whom He wants you to be a friend to, and you can ask the Holy Spirit to lead you to what He would have you do.

Honestly, I could fill a book with all the beautiful friends who in some way brought God's Word, love, and encouragement, and reminded me, "Hey, I'm here for you. I love you, and I'm praying for you." A little love goes a long way.

I'm thankful for these women, and I'm thankful for Ruth's example. I'm inspired to be the kind of friend I was born to be—one who reaches out, works hard, loves well, and lives beautifully.

Be a Catalyst

When we connect with one another with vulnerability, when we gather with the intent to lift each other up, to speak life, and to cheer each other on, something special happens. We empower one another to keep running, to keep growing, to keep blooming. We help unveil the truth that it's possible to flourish beautifully right where God has us.

Throughout my life, I have been surrounded by various crews of women, and I've needed each one in each season. My very first small group was led by my junior high youth pastor and his wife and included a few students. This time was so life-changing for me because of how much my leaders cared for me and spoke truth and life and purpose into my little sixth-grade bud of a life. I have been in small groups with women of a variety of ages and in a variety of seasons. I am the woman I am today, struggles and all, because of the women who have been in my life. And I am so thankful.

The Enemy hates it when women gather because he knows the implications of powerful women being in each other's corners. He knows that we're unstoppable when we're united and when we love and serve God together. That's why he does everything he can to try to keep us throwing jabs and punches at each other. Did you know that cats generally fight because of hormones, jealousy, or the need to protect their territory? That's why we can be called catty; it's harsh, but can be true! But it doesn't have to be said of us. It can be easy to throw out a snarky comment or put someone down in a passive-aggressive way. It's much harder to fight to be honorable, to believe the best about others and assume they're not out to hurt us.

When women gather, clothed in humility and honor, speaking life and love, it's a picture of Romans 12:9–11 in action:

> Let the inner movement of your heart always be to love one another, and never play the role of an actor wearing a mask. Despise evil and embrace everything that is good and virtuous.
>
> Be devoted to tenderly loving your fellow believers as members of one family. Try to outdo yourselves in respect and honor of one another.
>
> Be enthusiastic to serve the Lord, keeping your passion toward him boiling hot! Radiate with the glow of the Holy Spirit and let him fill you with excitement as you serve him. (TPT)

Letting the inner movement of our hearts be to love one another would change the trajectory of our lives. We could leave a trail of sweetness causing the gathering of ladies to be full of strength and peace. I want to keep fighting to be that kind of woman—a catalyst.

The word *catalyst* means "something that causes activity between two or more persons" and "a person whose talk, enthusiasm or energy causes others to be more friendly, enthusiastic or energetic." We are meant to be a catalyst to those around us, to live enthusiastically and energetically and in so doing enrich the atmosphere. Remember how I told you that God designed you for good and to bring good to the situations in your life? This is the catalyst you were born to be.

If we fight for our friendships, we can change our relationships and our lives. The Bible says that the righteous are as bold as a lion (Proverbs 28:1). You may not feel bold, but it is part of the flourishing picture that you are in Christ. You may not feel as though you're the kind of friend you are meant to be, but you're growing right now. Whether or not you see the change, God is working in you.

Leopards fascinate me. In the book *Death in the Long Grass*, I learned that "besides [her] incredible strength, the leopard moves at blinding speed from close quarters and is noted for her patience, calculating intelligence, hair-raising ferocity, and boldness wrapped in the best camouflage in nature beside a fashion model." How inspiring is this cat? I love another phrase the book used: "velvet-sheathed murder." In other words, leopards are tender and tough, sensitive and strong, compassionate and confident—just like the kind of woman you are meant to be.

A wounded leopard, however, is a dangerous animal. If it feels threatened, it will choose fight over flight. A ton of debris and bacteria build up under their curved nails, so even a small scratch from these cats could prove deadly.

I want to speak tenderly to you. Like the leopard, a wounded woman can be dangerous if she lets hurt, anger, pain, and frustration lead her relationships. But a wounded woman with a healthy soul, who is letting her Savior heal her, is a significant tool in God's hands. Instead of clawing others with her words or actions, she can strengthen those around her and point them to Jesus, His Word, and His church.

Just because you might be stuck *in* a struggle doesn't mean you'll always be stuck *with* this struggle. God is with you, and He is all you need. He is your strength and your perfect Father, and He has surrounded you with women to support you, to struggle with you, and to pray with you. You are not alone.

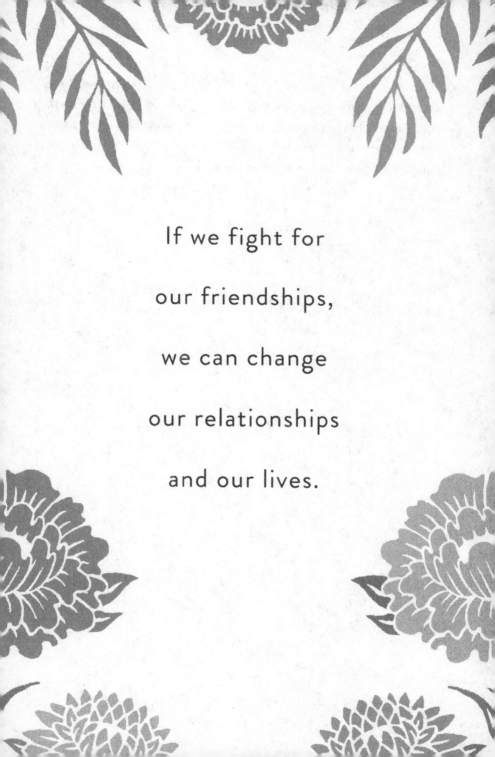

If we fight for

our friendships,

we can change

our relationships

and our lives.

I believe that as you cling tightly to Jesus, and as you reach out and see the women who are there for you and the ones who need you, you will be the catalyst you were created to be. You will see life through the lens of true friendship with your Creator and with your fellow fight club. We are stronger together.

13

The Silent Treatment

I'm so thankful that the Bible is full of different kinds of people with different kinds of challenges, personalities, backgrounds, and experiences. I don't see perfection; I see the failures, the humanity, the real-life struggle. I'm not the only one who has felt as though I'm not flourishing. I'm not the only one who has made huge messes that seem impossible to clean up. I'm not the only one who has tried to take matters into her own hands. If these real-life people with real-life messes are in the Bible, it reminds me I'm not alone in this fight. And it encourages me that flourishing looks different for everyone. I can pause, take a deep breath, and take another step.

There are so many examples of women who were fearless in the face of adversity and courageous when no one else would step up to the plate—Ruth, Deborah, and Mary, to name a few. And then there are other women who displayed more of the selfish, prideful, and sinful side of humanity. They may not be as inspiring, but I find that I can relate more to their failures and struggles.

I'm thinking of women like Sarah. Until recently, I've never had a desire to study her life. She's not someone I had ever particularly admired or considered strong, brave, or kind. When I looked more closely, however, I sensed a depth I had never noticed before. I related to her and empathized with her life.

When Sarah makes her debut in the book of Genesis, we discover that her OG name was Sarai. (God later changed her name to Sarah, so that's what I'll call her.) And she was barren. In a day when bearing children was a sign of blessing and fruitfulness, she was a sixty-five-year-old infertile woman. She didn't have much hope of birthing a baby. My heart broke for her.

I've never been in that position, so I don't understand the heartache of trying but not being able to become pregnant. I've also never experienced the death of a child inside my womb, though I have walked with a few friends who have gone through this kind of pain. Both circumstances bring great loss and heartbreak. Whether a woman suffers a miscarriage or loss of a child or struggles with infertility, she can't help but grieve what could have been.

I often wonder what Lenya would be like if she were still with us. As of the writing of this book, she would be twelve and in the sixth grade. If she was like me, she would have already started her period and would be blooming into a young woman. Would she have kept her hair long and wild, or would she have cut it short? Would she have tried gymnastics and loved it? Would she be learning jiu jitsu along with her sisters? Which Impact team would she serve with at church? What would life be like today if she was with us? I hate that I'll never know.

Sarah was at an age when she could have been a grandmother. Perhaps her family members and friends were in that stage of life, but she didn't have children, let alone grandchildren. I imagine she was a loving aunt to her nephew Lot. Perhaps she also spent time with the young women in her community, teaching them how to cook, how to be good wives, and what she knew of this new God in their lives.

As I read about Sarah, I noticed the Bible doesn't mention a single instance of God speaking directly to her. That doesn't mean that He never did, but only the conversations between God and Abraham are recorded. In Genesis 15, God gave Abraham the promise that he and Sarah were going to have a son. About ten years passed, and they still had no children.

So Sarah came up with a desperate and crazy idea. She told Abraham, "Look. My womb is clearly not working. You should have sex with my young and fertile maid, Hagar. Maybe this is the way we'll have kids."

What does Abraham say? "Sure honey, whatever you say" (Genesis 16:2, my paraphrase). Of course he did!

What unfolded from this moment was painful and complicated for all involved. When Hagar got pregnant, she despised Sarah, and I sympathize with her. Sarah then blamed Abraham, though the whole plan was her idea, and mistreated Hagar, who ran away and came back after God told her to. Hagar gave birth to a son, Ishmael, but he was not the son God promised Abraham. So Sarah was right back where she started, only she was older and dealing with a family mess she created.

I don't know how Sarah felt at that point, but I imagine she was pretty disheartened. God had given her an amazing promise, but so many years had gone by and she still didn't have a kid. Why was God so silent? I wonder if Sarah had given up believing.

Thirteen years after Ishmael's birth, God appeared to Abraham again. Once again, He didn't talk to Sarah but to her husband. She overheard the conversation, and when God said she would give birth to a son the following year, she laughed (Genesis 18:12). We don't know exactly why she laughed. Maybe it was more of a sarcastic snicker because she had lost hope at that point. That's probably what I would have done.

It seems like this is often how God rolls in the Bible. He gives a promise and then goes off the grid. It's as though the person on the receiving end says into a walkie-talkie, "Come in, God. Come in. Are you there?" And in return, there's nothing but static. Silence. Crickets.

I used to think that Sarah was weak and distrusting when she took her situation into her own hands and arranged for Abraham and Hagar to have a baby. But I do see where she was coming from. She wanted to do God's will, but nothing was making sense or going in that direction, so she thought she'd help. I do the same thing. (Well, not that *exact* thing.) I tend to try to do God's will in my own way and in my own timing. If I don't hear from God, I often move forward with my own plan.

When You Don't Hear a Thing

The Bible says that God is near to the brokenhearted, to those who are crushed in spirit (Psalm 34:18). When Lenya went to heaven these were words that described me—*brokenhearted* and *crushed*. Yet in this unrelenting ache, I felt God's nearness and His peace like never before. It's as if the curtain between earth and heaven opened and a breeze from heaven blew down to earth, leaving an imprint on everyone left behind.

After Lenya left, months stretched into years, and our family settled into a new and different normal. I still felt the ache of her absence—and I also felt a distance between God and me. I didn't feel as near to heaven as I had in the early days of her death.

I felt as if God were giving me the silent treatment. The silent treatment is generally a negative behavior, usually an unhealthy response to conflict paired with anger and resentment. We as women tend to be professionals in the prescription of this treatment.

In this season, I did the same things I had always done to grow in my relationship with God. I prayed. I read the Bible. I gathered with my church family. I worshiped. I served. I gave. Nothing had changed except for the development of what felt like a chasm between me and God. He felt far away.

I discovered that, as in any relationship, there are ebbs and flows of connectedness in our relationship with God. If you're married, you know that you're not always going to feel the rush of adrenaline like you did when you first held hands when you were dating. Or how you felt on your wedding night. Yet, there's a deepening that happens over time when you continue to honor and prefer each other, whether or not you feel the thrill.

The truth was, even though I didn't feel God at the time, He was still there with me. He didn't leave my corner. He wasn't angry with me. And He didn't forget about me.

Levi and I recently traveled together without the kids. As our plane descended, I looked out the window and saw a low-hanging, dense blanket of dark clouds. It looked like a rain storm. Then, the first ray of sunlight poked through. It brought such hope to my heart. And because I didn't have Lennox to hold, and my laptop was stored away for landing, and I hadn't brought a book, I just sat there staring out the tiny window. By the time the dark clouds had finished dissolving, the most beautiful sky I had ever seen revealed itself. I had seen only the darkness, what separated me from the sunshine. But as the sun broke through, I could see its warmth and beauty.

This experience reminded me of what God is doing in the background. Even if we can't see what He's doing or hear His voice, He's still there. God hasn't turned His back; He is giving us space to trust Him.

Drop the Dead Weight

God's love for us is never dependent on what we do. He loves us unconditionally and deeply and perfectly. I think that's sometimes hard to understand because of our experience with people who make us feel as though we need to earn God's love. And through that lens, it's easy to believe that if God doesn't speak to us, it's because we did something wrong and He has turned His back on us. But the truth is that God hasn't left us. He hasn't forsaken us. He's not mad at us. God looks at us only with love in His eyes.

I have had a hard time accepting this truth. I've thought that if I do good, then God will love me more. If I do bad, God will reject me. But it isn't the truth. We have to fight to see how God views us and how He treats us. Here's a clue from Psalm 103:2–5:

> Bless the LORD, O my soul,
> And forget not all His benefits:
> Who forgives all your iniquities,
> Who heals all your diseases,
> Who redeems your life from destruction,
> Who crowns you with lovingkindness and tender mercies,
> Who satisfies your mouth with good things,
> So that your youth is renewed like the eagle's.

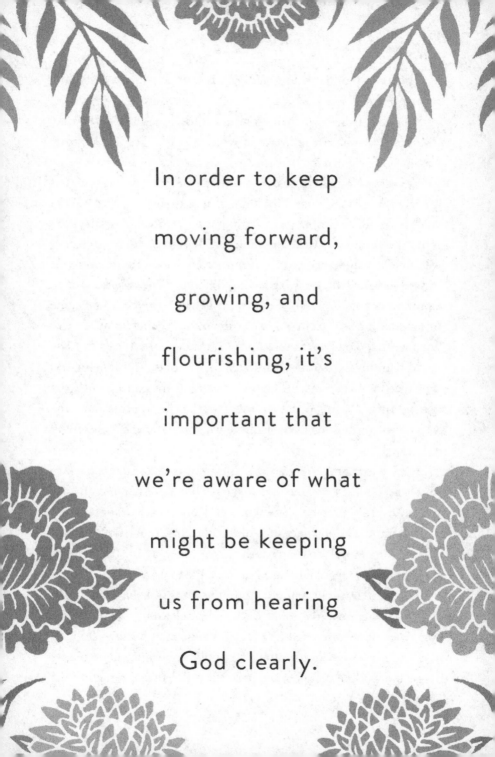

In order to keep
moving forward,
growing, and
flourishing, it's
important that
we're aware of what
might be keeping
us from hearing
God clearly.

The heart of God is to forgive, heal, redeem, crown, satisfy, and renew.

In order to keep moving forward, growing, and flourishing, it's important that we're aware of what might be keeping us from hearing God clearly. It's true that sin can hold us back from hearing the next step God has for us. As the writer of Hebrews said, "Let us lay aside every weight, and the sin which so easily ensnares us, and let us run with endurance the race that is set before us, looking unto Jesus, the author and finisher of our faith" (12:1–2). It's possible that we can allow sin to keep us from running toward a flourishing life.

If God is silent, or we're feeling like there's not a clear line of communication, it could be that we're getting tripped up on some things holding us back in our lives. I'm not saying that because we've done wrong, God won't speak to us. But I do want to say that His Word reminds us to walk with, listen to, and obey Him. If God has set a race for us to run, if He has set before us the picture of Christ that we are becoming like, then there will be checkpoints along the way, opportunities for us to shed the weight that might be keeping us back.

My houseplants—or happy plants, as I like to call them—are very dear to me. I love how they make my home fresher and greener and an overall happier place. I'm not a houseplant expert, but I understand the importance of pruning. Recently I took out my mini shears, mini shovel, dusting brush, and mini spray-mister (I might not be a houseplant expert, but I do have the tools of one) so I could cut away dead leaves and stems and cultivate the soil. *Snip. Snip. Snip.*

Or maybe more like, *hack, hack, hack*, at least in my daughters' eyes. They were concerned I was cutting too much. When I stopped to admire my work, I admitted they might be right. Some plants barely looked like plants at all, just stubs. But then I remembered why I snipped in the first place: the dead parts were keeping these plants from growing.

We can ask God to show us what holds us back and stunts our growth. Psalm 139:23–24 says it best:

> God, see what is in my heart.
>> Know what is there.
> Test me.
>> Know what I'm thinking.
>> See if there's anything in my life you don't like.
>> Help me live in the way that is always right. (NIrv)

Sometimes we can be ignorant of our own blind spots. We can keep fighting to flourish and not see what's weighing us down. It's a healthy practice to let God survey our souls. When we ask Him, He will lovingly show us what we can drop so that we can run.

A friend of mine has an incredible green thumb, evident by her gorgeous garden. I asked her what she's learned about the blooming of her flowers. Her answer was stunning. She told me the lessons God has taught her over time have very little to do with their blooms. Instead, pruning, plucking out weeds, and regular watering have brought her the most growth.

We as a culture put such an emphasis on blooming. We've heard it said, "Bloom where you're planted." The idea being—or the picture on Pinterest showing—that if you're in the desert, bloom there; if you're in a rocky place, bloom there. But instead of focusing on blooming where we're planted, which can happen in its time but is fleeting, we should prune where we're planted. Weed where we're planted. Water where we're planted.

We prune plants because we know that they won't thrive if

they're carrying dead weight. God does the same with us. There are some things, or even people, He needs to pluck away. It can be a painful process.

Farther down in Hebrews 12, the writer said, "No chastening seems to be joyful for the present, but painful; nevertheless, afterward it yields the peaceable fruit of righteousness to those who have been trained by it" (12:11). Discipline is never fun. But what if we looked at it as a method of training? When God chastens us through pruning or weeding, think of it as a good thing. It may hurt and seem unfair, but it produces in us a growth and fruit that wouldn't have come otherwise. Let's seek to be trainable while we're planted in a hard season and to be open to God showing us what may be holding us back or weighing us down.

Safe in His Shadow

It's funny to me how the Bible compares us to sheep. It's not really a compliment because sheep are hard to lead. They're easily frightened, they tend to have friction with other sheep, and they just don't know what they need. (Kinda sounds like me, to be honest.) Sheep need someone to lead them, and so do we. Psalm 23 tells us who the best person for the job is: "The LORD is my shepherd; I shall not want. He makes me to lie down in green pastures; He leads me beside the still waters. He restores my soul" (vv. 1–3).

If we trust that the Lord is our shepherd, then we can know we're right where we need to be. This knowledge yields confidence. Our Shepherd is our leader, and if we stick close to Him, He will faithfully lead us and give us the instructions for our next steps.

When I let God lead me, He gives me everything I need. He

leads me step-by-step because He wants us to keep running to Him and walking with Him. If we look to Him—even in His seeming absence—He won't lead us in the wrong way but in the best way.

Psalm 23 also says, "Yea, though I walk through the valley of the shadow of death, I will fear no evil; for You are with me" (v. 4). That sounds really scary. Why would God lead us *into* the valley of the shadow of death? I'm not sure, though I know that death is a part of life on earth. And I know that no matter what we walk through, God is with us. Even when we feel alone, even when we feel our Shepherd has vanished, He has His eyes on His sheep.

We might not be able to see Him in the shadows, but He sees us.

> He who dwells in the secret place of the Most High
> Shall abide under the shadow of the Almighty.
> I will say of the LORD, "He is my refuge and my fortress;
> My God, in Him I will trust."
> He shall cover you with His feathers,
> And under His wings you shall take refuge. (Psalm 91:1–2, 4)

The next time you feel like God is far way and you're alone in the dark, picture yourself in the shadow of His wings. He's nearer than He seems. He loves you more than you know. The darkness doesn't mean He's gone; it means He's close and holding you near. You are safe in His shadow.

The Gift of the Test

The Scholastic Assessment Test (SAT, also known as my nemesis in high school) is now a faint reminder of failure. I was a good student;

I got decent grades, and I tested well. When it came to the SAT, however, I felt like I didn't know a single thing. The first time I took the test, I got a 980 out of 1600. I took it again and my score was worse—a 930. I'm ashamed that I'm apparently not super bright in the SAT world.

Test-taking is hard. There's so much pressure: the quiet room, the ticking clock, the teacher sitting there with a look on her face that says, *Good luck. Your whole future depends on this moment right here. No pressure, kid.*

The Bible gives us great advice when we encounter a test:

> Consider it a sheer gift, friends, when tests and challenges come
> at you from all sides. You know that under pressure, your faith-
> life is forced into the open and shows its true colors. So don't
> try to get out of anything prematurely. Let it do its work so you
> become mature and well-developed, not deficient in any way.
> (James 1:2–4 THE MESSAGE)

Trials and tests are gifts? Yes. If we run away from our struggles or choose to numb the pain instead of feeling it, we're not letting the pressure of the test do its beautifying work in our lives.

God designed you to walk through the pain. He knows that on the other side, you'll find strength, character, and maturity. The test is a gift; the process is valuable. Keep putting your faith into practice and watch as God strengthens you and causes you to flourish in the struggle.

When God is silent, it's not the time to panic or give up. Press into the resistance. Keep believing. Keep trusting. My friend Alex Seeley once told me while we were hiking in Glacier National Park, "When you feel spiritually dry or far from God, dig deep ditches.

When God is silent, it's not the time to panic or give up. Press into the resistance. Keep believing. Keep trusting.

Lean into God's Word even more. Pour your heart out before Him. Write out your prayers. When you dig a little deeper in times of drought, when God shows up and rains down, the ditches you dug in the dryness will fill up with water, and refreshing, and blessing."

Remember Sarah? In the midst of the heartache and difficulty, God's promise was fulfilled through her, and she had a baby—*the* baby God said she would have. It's hard to show up when you feel like God is ghosting you. But by now we know we're not expecting easy. One of the most significant things we can do during a trial is to take a second look at it through the lens of faith.

Take Another Look

When you're overwhelmed by the silent treatment, look again. God may have seemed silent throughout Sarah's life. But her story doesn't end with her death at age 127. She's mentioned again in the New Testament in an incredible list of spiritual giants highlighted for their faith.

> By faith Sarah herself also received strength to conceive seed, and she bore a child when she was past the age, because she judged Him faithful who had promised. Therefore from one man, and him as good as dead, were born as many as the stars of the sky in multitude—innumerable as the sand which is by the seashore. (Hebrews 11:11–12)

I don't know every detail of Sarah's story, but this glimpse into her heart fascinates me: *By faith Sarah herself also received strength.* Sarah's not just part of this story; she was needed as part of the recipe for this miracle. Without her, the child God promised to her and Abraham wouldn't exist. The key phrase here: *she judged Him faithful who had promised.* Whatever her struggle had been to believe God, the headline over her life was that she judged Him faithful, even in the silence.

The silent treatment may be painful, confusing, and harsh. But look again—this time with the eyes to see that this test will bring the maturity, the power, and the life you were meant to have. It will be a challenge to see the struggle for what it really is, but the only way to truly flourish is to fight forward and to see what God sees— Christ in you.

A seed is planted deep in the soil, far from sunshine and from everything warm and good. Yet the darkness and distance serve a purpose. They create the space needed for growth and maturity. We are very much like seeds in this way. When we feel separated or disconnected from God, we're living in the tension of sanctification, the process between believing in Jesus now and seeing Him later. When we continue to trust Him in the silence, we'll discover that we're actually flourishing in His shadow.

14

Shake Up the Freshness

One year, Levi bought me a juicer for my birthday. I was really into green juice and drinking my salad, so I was excited to make my own juice from organic fruits and veggies. I knew it was going to be a commitment of my time and our money, but I was ready.

I did it consistently for a year—and then I got tired of it. I got tired of the forty-five minutes it took me to wash, cut, and juice the produce and clean the juicer. Then one day we put the juicer away because it took up too much counter space. It stayed away for a long time, maybe a year. Now the juicer makes an appearance every so often. In fact, just the other day my daughters asked to juice. My response? "Sorry, kids; ain't nobody got time for such a thing." For the most part, home juicing and my life aren't currently on speaking terms.

If you juice at home or buy fresh juices from the market, you might have noticed that the liquid separates. The lighter part at the top is the water that makes up most of these drinks. The darker part at the bottom, called the sediment, contains all the nutrients and vitamins. This separation is a sign that the juice was made without added chemicals, fillers, or binders, which is healthier for you.

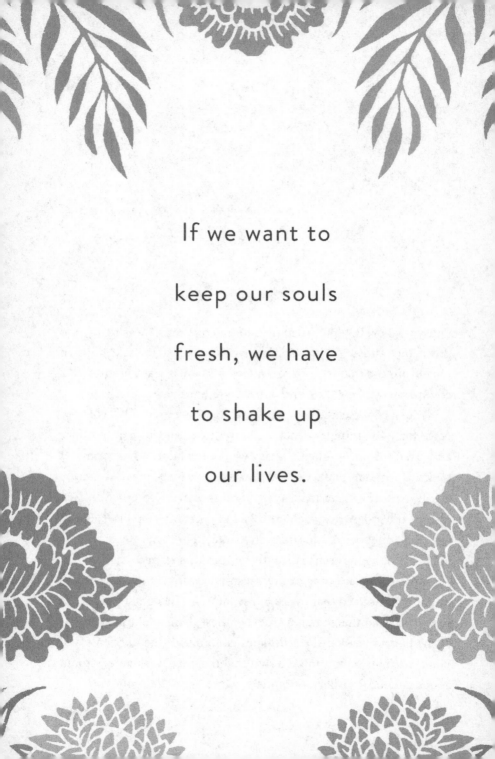

If we want to

keep our souls

fresh, we have

to shake up

our lives.

But you don't want to drink your juice when it's separated like that. You'll need to first give it a good shake. In fact, many juices have labels that read something like "Separation is natural—shake it up!" or "Shake vigorously to enjoy fully." You could drink the juice separated, but it wouldn't taste great, and the nutrients would stay stuck at the bottom and not make it into your body. If you want to get the most out of your healthy beverage, it has to be shaken up.

Similarly, if we want to keep our souls fresh, we have to shake up our lives. Sometimes we're the ones who decide to shake things up, and sometimes God does it for us.

When I was nineteen, I knew something needed to change in my life. I'd graduated high school and ended a serious relationship, and something in my soul needed a little shake-up. So I packed up my mattress and a few boxes of belongings and moved from Monterey, California, to Albuquerque, New Mexico, to serve as an intern with the missions department at a church. I also made the decision then to not date for a year.

But I met Levi halfway through that year, and he had made no such commitment. So here we were, serving God together in the student ministry. We liked each other, but there was nothing we could do about it. Even though he didn't like it, Levi honored my decision, and we stayed friends—nothing more, nothing less.

Looking back, I couldn't have orchestrated it better myself. God did it, and I'm so thankful for that. Having that guideline of no dating for a year forced me to focus in a way that I may not have otherwise. It was what Levi and I both needed, and God knew that.

The night my internship ended, Levi asked me out on our first date. My life has been forever changed for the better because God shook up my life in a way only He could.

When Spiritual Separation Leads to a Spiritual Rut

If we're left to our own plans or get too comfortable, we're going to drift off course. Unfortunately, we never drift in the right direction. Maybe we spend less time in God's Word than we should, or we lean on our own strength instead of being dependent on Him. We get a little lazy and forget how important it is to keep our guard up. We let our tiredness dictate our actions. Our punches get weaker and not as accurate. We can lose the desire to fight with a little fire under our feet.

Our hearts, when left to themselves, start to divide their attention. We start letting things steal our focus away from God. Our hearts can be sneaky opponents. If we're not careful, we can be tricked into thinking that we're doing well, when in reality, we're not. We're distracted. We're busy. We're not focused on the One we can't live without—Jesus. Before we know it, the bell rings, eight rounds are over, and we've lost the match. We're left with dull lives, not the vibrant ones we're meant to live.

I'd like to think the writer of Psalm 86:11 understood the reality of spiritual separation when he wrote, "Teach me Your way, O Lord; I will walk in Your truth; Unite my heart to fear Your name."

Unite my heart.

For uniting to take place, division must have happened. When my heart separates itself and divides its focus, I pray, *God, unite my heart to fear Your name.*

One book that has really stirred my heart is A. W. Tozer's *Rut, Rot, or Revival.* He wrote, "When we come to the place where everything can be predicted and nobody expects anything unusual from God, we are in a rut."

A rut is "a fixed or established mode of procedure or course of life, usually dull or unpromising." *Dull* and *unpromising* are not words I want to describe my life. But I often feel like I am not living the vibrant, gorgeous, stunning life I think I should be, mostly because I'm comparing myself to others. I find myself saying, "I wish my life was as glamorous as hers." Or "I would do everything she does if I had her means and resources." When we play the comparison game, we can easily find ourselves in a rut. I love this quote I saw on my friend's Instagram feed: "A flower does not think of competing with the flower next to it. It just blooms."

Tozer knew the dangers that come with falling into a spiritual rut. He wrote, "Complacency is a deadly foe of all spiritual growth. Acute desire must be present or there will be no manifestation of Christ to His people. He waits to be wanted. Too bad that with many of us He waits so long, so very long, in vain."

We have the choice to let Jesus shake us up or to stay in our comfort zones. Not looking to Jesus, not letting Him change us with His Word and with the trials we face, keeps us stagnant. We won't grow and we won't mature.

But the good news is that we can do something about it.

When you vigorously shake a natural juice, the separation goes away. The good stuff doesn't stay at the bottom, and the bland stuff doesn't stay at the top. The sediment and water blend.

Allowing God to shake us up is truly fresh living. One of the definitions of *fresh* is "brisk; vigorous; not tired or fatigued." When we fight to keep Jesus our focus, fresh growth can happen. As we encounter tests or trials, we can let Him water us and prune back what we don't need so we can continue to grow. My prayer is that you and I would always be in a place where we allow God to do the work in us that He wants to, and that we would always give the Holy Spirit an all-access pass to our lives.

Aging Beautifully

Breaking news: we're all getting older. When I see a gray hair on my head, my first impulse is to pluck it out and hijack the signs of aging, but there's no stopping it. I know, it's not super encouraging, but it's the truth.

Here's the breaking *good news*: "Even though our outward man is perishing, yet the inward man is being renewed day by day" (2 Corinthians 4:16). Something beautiful happens as we age. We undergo a deepening, a strengthening, a growth, a beauty that no glamour magazine can photograph.

The magic of a flourishing life, no matter how old we are, is this: we are becoming more like Jesus every day. But I know how hard it is to see this with our natural eyes (which are also fading, by the way). So we power on the lens of faith to see the beautiful work happening within us.

Psalm 92:14 says the righteous "shall still bear fruit in old age; they shall be fresh and flourishing." This brings me so much hope. In Christ, the older I get, the stronger I get.

I know many older women who age beautifully. They have a strength and a grace and a grit that no amount of money can buy, no anti-aging creams can produce. Every one of these women has experienced hard things, but they've let the hard things do the hard work in their souls.

We have the potential to grow stronger and more kindhearted as we age. Look at Elizabeth, whom we meet in Luke 1. Elizabeth and her husband, Zacharias, were a power couple. Zacharias was a priest, and Elizabeth was born from a priestly lineage. "They were both righteous before God, walking in all the commandments and ordinances of the Lord blameless" (v. 6). Then comes a "but," a pretty big one: "*But* they had no child, because Elizabeth was barren, and they were both well advanced in years" (v. 7, emphasis mine). *Well advanced in years*. Well, that's a nice way to say saggy and wrinkly.

And yet, Zacharias continued to serve God as a priest even when he and his wife struggled with their infertility (v. 8). It's easy to let difficulties keep us from gathering with God's people and serving in the church, but He will fashion a deep work in us and will impact others through us if we keep showing up. When we give in the midst of grief, when we serve in the midst of suffering, when we are active in the midst of the ache, beautiful things happen.

This couple had a big *but* (a big obstacle) in their lives, but here comes an even bigger and better *but*, in which God stepped into an impossible situation: "An angel of the Lord appeared to [Zacharias]. . . . *But* the angel said to him, 'Do not be afraid, Zacharias, for your prayer is heard; and your wife Elizabeth will bear you a son, and you shall call his name John'" (vv. 11, 13, emphasis mine).

Zacharias didn't believe the news, so the angel basically told him, "Dude, I'm Gabriel. I'm an angel. I hang out with God all the time. He was the one who told me to tell you this. What's your problem, man? Now, because you didn't believe me, you won't speak till the baby comes" (vv. 19–20, my paraphrase). Oops.

What happens later in their story is so wonderful. An angel appeared to Mary, a relative of Elizabeth's, who was pregnant at the time with Jesus. The angel told Mary about Elizabeth's pregnancy: "Elizabeth your relative has also conceived a son in her old age; and this is now the sixth month for her who was called barren. For with God nothing will be impossible" (vv. 36–37).

The angel told Mary she was going to have a baby, that her older cousin Elizabeth was having a baby, and that with God nothing will be impossible. It was true then, and it's true today.

When Mary visited with Elizabeth after hearing the good news, Elizabeth greeted her in such a special way:

> "Blessed are you among women, and blessed is the fruit of your womb! But why is this granted to me, that the mother of my Lord should come to me? For indeed, as soon as the voice of your greeting sounded in my ears, the babe leaped in my womb for joy. Blessed is she who believed, for there will be a fulfillment of those things which were told her from the Lord." (vv. 42–45).

Elizabeth had a beautiful grace about her. Like Sarah, I'm sure she had mourned the loss of what could have been. She must have been happy for her friends when they had babies, throwing baby shower after baby shower, even as she wondered when her time would come.

Because Elizabeth believed God and allowed Him to accomplish His will in His time—shaking up her life in the process—she gave birth to the man who would pave the way for Jesus. Thirtysome years later, Jesus said about Elizabeth's son, "Among those born of women there is not a greater prophet than John the Baptist" (Luke 7:28). It might have taken Elizabeth a long time to have a child, but when God brought her a baby, he was the OG G.O.A.T.

Fresh Life

Loving and serving God and others takes effort and persistence and grit. This is the heart of our home and our church, Fresh Life. Even before Levi and I moved to Montana, before we had the privilege of leading this church, we believe God gave us this name.

My husband and I were sitting in the Salt Lake City airport with Alivia, who was thirteen months old. We had been asking God if we should move from California to Montana. In fact, earlier that morning, while visiting Montana, Levi had prayed, "God, if you give us a name for this church before we get back to California today, a name that we don't just like but that we love, we'll move to Montana." (Hello, bold prayer!)

At that point, we had nothing. No names, not even an idea for one. At the airport, Levi asked me, "What do you think God wants to do in the Flathead Valley?" (At the time, this region of the state was what was on our radar. We didn't know our church would eventually have sites all over the state of Montana and beyond, including in Utah, Oregon, and Wyoming.)

"It seems like God wants to breathe fresh life in this valley," I replied.

We looked at each other with a sparkle in our eyes, and I said, "Fresh Life? Fresh Life Church?"

It was such a good name. No, it was the *best* name. We thought for sure there was already a church called Fresh Life somewhere in the world. But when we searched Google, we found nothing. We couldn't believe it. This name was too good for it to not already be a thing. Levi immediately bought the domain names for FreshLifeChurch.org and FreshLifeChurch.com, closed our laptop, and said with confidence, "Well, I guess we're moving to Montana."

We didn't just like the name; we loved it. And it didn't reflect just an idea but a way of living. We said yes to God without knowing what was in store for us.

God calls us to live fresh lives, not stagnant ones, and to be fruitful in all seasons. Build up your expectations; it could be just another day, month, or year for you—or it could be the best of your

Impossible

is His

favorite

thing to

work with.

life. When you're tired, when you're weak, when you feel like your situation is impossible, remember that God is working in you. And remember that impossible is His favorite thing to work with.

Keep Your Chin Up

Chuck "The Iceman" Liddell was the first UFC superstar, the best in the world at his job. Levi and I have had the privilege of meeting him and his family, and they have also been to our church. Recently, I watched a fascinating special about this man of strength.

Chuck's trainer said, "Chuck never really cared about being a fighter, he just loved to fight. . . . Chuck was always a tough, durable guy who could hit hard, kick hard, and had a great takedown defense. And the one thing that enabled him to do all that was his unbelievable chin. Age gets us all . . . I realized [Chuck] lost his chin, and once you lose your chin, it's gone." In fighting, the phrase "lose your chin" means losing the ability to fight because you can't take a punch anymore. There came a point when the Iceman couldn't take a hit like he used to.

The key is to allow ourselves to be shaken up but not be taken down. To let life hit us but to keep our chins; to let life punch us but not to be knocked out. Even if we feel we've failed, we've got to be able to take the punches so we can keep fighting forward and flourishing until we see Jesus face-to-face.

Keep your chin by looking up. When your world is shaken—whether for better or for worse—keep your eyes on the One who is in the fight with you. Psalm 121:1–2 says, "I lift up my eyes to the mountains—where does my help come from? My help comes from the Lord, the Maker of heaven and earth" (NIV).

I heard an analogy when I was a little girl that has stuck with me my whole life. Our lives are like a parade. It has a beginning and an end, and because we're marching in the parade, we can't see what's behind us or what's in front of us. We can only see what we're in right now. God is like a helicopter hovering above the action, with the whole parade in view. He sees the turns we'll have to take, the potholes we'll have to jump over, the slippery stretches that might make us fall, the buildings that tower over us casting shadows.

As we experience events or circumstances that shake us up, we have to remember to look up. We may not be able to see from God's perspective, but we can trust that He sees. And as the book of James reminds us, our lives are like a vapor (4:14), so before we know it, we'll be at the end of the parade and in heaven with Jesus and those we love.

When we allow God to shake up the freshness in us, we are able to see the obstacles, the struggles, the joys, and the pains as fertilizer that gives us the nutrients we need to keep growing in the right direction.

Most trees grow in the same direction: up. But then there are the trees that grow on the tiny piece of land at the southern tip of New Zealand's South Island. Because of the severe Antarctic winds, these trees grow sideways, as though a giant hair dryer were blowing them in that direction. They remind me of what Paul wrote: "We are hard-pressed on every side, yet not crushed; we are perplexed, but not in despair; persecuted, but not forsaken; struck down, but not destroyed—always carrying about in the body the dying of the Lord Jesus, that the life of Jesus also may be manifested in our body" (2 Corinthians 4:8–10).

These trees may not look like typical trees to us, but they're growing. We may feel battered by extreme winds, but we can still thrive. We may be bruised, but we can still flourish. The trees in my backyard might look different from yours, but they're growing just the same.

Recently, Levi and I were driving around vineyards, and it was interesting to see how different the vines grew. Some grew outward with their grapes hanging high, ready to be picked. But others drooped down to the ground, their grapes almost grazing the dirt. Some looked a bit messier than others, but each vine was fulfilling its purpose.

The same is true for you. Your growth will look different from others'. Your life may look a little crooked or uneven or droopy, but you're still growing. Your life may feel a little more shaken than others, but you're still standing.

Being shaken up isn't comfortable or easy, but it's necessary. We can't vibrantly flourish unless we're shaken. And the only way to survive that shaking is to remember that God is with us. Dear friend, with Him nothing is impossible.

15

Show Up and Stand Out

I don't travel by myself very often. When I have to fly alone, Levi and I start cracking jokes. Will I make it there alive? Will I know how to Uber? Will I find my hotel? While I may be travel-challenged, I'll have you know that I have made it to my destination and back successfully every time. Go me!

On one particular solo trip, I was heading back home from New York. I didn't need to study or work on a message, so the flight felt like a luxury. I could watch a movie or TV show, read, sleep, or listen to music. There were no screaming babies in my lap. I had even been upgraded.

I was living the life.

When mealtime rolled around, I was excited to eat while watching a movie. Just before diving into the steaming tray, I felt a tap on my shoulder. I pulled my headphones aside and looked at the older gentleman sitting next to me.

"It's dinnertime," he said with a smile. "Time to put the technology away."

I thought, *Did I hear him right?*

"Excuse me?" I replied, trying to hide my bewilderment.

"Let's be human and have a human conversation." For the record, we hadn't said much to each other before this except for an exchange of hellos when he sat down next to me during boarding.

Still somewhat shocked but willing to give it a go, I responded, "Why yes, of course!"

When I sit next to people I don't know, I generally keep my headphones and phone off until they enter into their own world with a book or digital entertainment. I keep my listening ears available in case they want to talk. I've had some incredible airplane conversations in which I've shared my story and the gospel and listened to others' stories, but no one had ever taken the reins to my in-flight meal service.

My seatmate and I had a pretty great conversation. Being well advanced in his years, he had a ton of neat stories and experiences to share. I told him about how our family ended up in Montana, about our daughter Lenya, and about God's faithfulness. By the time I had swallowed the last bite of my meal, I was thankful he had interrupted my "me time."

Through this experience, God reminded me of the importance of not just showing up but being fully present in a moment. When we turn up and stand out, God often has something special for us and for someone through us. You don't have to push a conversation on every person you bump into, but try to be open to conversations and connections God might be opening up right in front of you.

Front-Row Living

Speaking of what's in front of us, what comes to mind when you think of the front row? Sitting in the front row in school? Trying to find parking in the front row at the mall? Getting stuck in the front row at the movie theater? Let's consider how the front row may be just what you need to take yourself to the next level.

If you had asked me in high school about the front row, I would've said the smart people who have all the answers sit there. I usually tried to hide somewhere in the middle so teachers wouldn't call on me, especially in math class. I loved to learn but didn't like giving answers if I wasn't sure what they were. I probably would have admitted that the front row intimidated me and maybe even scared me a little.

Today, the front row is my favorite. When I reserve my bike in the front row at spin class, I know full well that I'm choosing an extra challenge and that I better bring my A game. The instructor can see me clearly, failures and all. This is scary, but it also brings a level of accountability, leadership, and expectation. I'm going to give my all, follow the instructor the best I can, and lead the people behind me well. I love this challenge. I don't nail every standing sprint or movement on the bike, but I do get stronger.

Don't just show up; show up with a mind-set to work hard, lean in, and put in the extra effort. This means doing what's difficult even when you face resistance. When you ride a spin bike, you control your own resistance. This is a good thing because you control your own workout—but it can also be a not-so-good thing because you control your own workout. Resistance is good for you because it helps your body fight a little harder and build stamina, strength, and endurance. We can grow by leaning in to the resistance and front-row pressure.

Similarly, there's something special about sitting in the front row in church. Something happens there that's hard to get in the back. I'm not saying that if you sit elsewhere you don't get anything out of the service; after all, someone has to sit in the back and in the middle. But worshiping in the front row—with hands raised, bright lights in your eyes, the bass and drums thumping in your soul—is unique. When you lean in to the message from the front row, it's as if you can feel a stretch on the inside, a posture of anticipation for what God has for you.

Paul wrote to the Thessalonian church this message: "And you became followers of my example and the Lord's when you received the word with the joy of the Holy Spirit, even though it resulted in tremendous trials and persecution. Now you have become an example for all the believers to follow throughout the provinces of Greece" (1 Thessalonians 1:6–7 TPT). This church had been through a lot. But as they followed Paul and followed Jesus, they received the Word with joy and readiness. And then they became an example to everyone living in Greece. If that's not front-row leadership, I don't know what is.

It's possible to be a poser in the front row, to do things just to do them. But pairing front-row living with the heart and energy and sweat and readiness that comes from within your soul—that's where the life-change happens.

Wake Up and Pay Attention

The book of 2 Kings tells a story about an unnamed woman. Or rather, she had a name—we just don't get the honor of knowing it until we get to heaven. Elisha, who was a prophet (a guy who spoke what was on God's heart to His people), often stopped by Shunem, the town where this woman and her husband lived. The woman invited the prophet over for a meal whenever he came around.

One day, the woman nudged her husband and said, "That man often comes by here. I know that he is a holy man of God. Let's make a small room for him on the roof. We'll put a bed and a table in it. We'll also put a chair and a lamp in it. Then he can stay there when he comes to visit us" (2 Kings 4:9–10 NIrv).

We don't know much about this woman other than that she was prominent in her community. But one of the things I notice about her is that she was present and attuned to others' needs.

I can picture her sitting in her home, reading the most recent issue of her favorite magazine, getting inspiration for her house, her garden, her life. As she gazes out the window in a daydream, she sees someone in the distance. When he's close enough, she recognizes him. Leaping from her chair, she bolts out the door to see him. She greets Elisha and urges him to stay for a meal. She sees a need and jumps at the chance to meet it.

Being aware and paying attention are two of the key ingredients to meeting people's needs.

I sometimes get overwhelmed when I see that there are so many people with so many needs. I am just one person; I can't do everything. That's a reason why I love the church. Being planted in the house and giving generously to the local church is so important; we can do so much more together than we can by ourselves.

Levi and I picked up this helpful tip from pastor Andy Stanley: "Do for one what you wish you could do for everyone." I try to keep this in mind when I have coffee with someone who is going through a difficult time. I can't meet with everyone, but I can meet this one person and commit to making the most out of our time together.

It's important to be generous and give to the church and charities. It's just as important to invest in the people closest to us, to give sacrificially of ourselves to our spouses, our children, our small groups. To see their needs and love them with God's love, all the more when we don't feel like it. This notable woman from 2 Kings didn't let people walk by without taking time to care for them. She noticed those around her and reached out in the way she could.

Be a Storyteller

I don't know what the hotel situation looked like in Elisha's days, but this woman refused to push Elisha's lodging needs on anyone else. She didn't make reservations for him at the nearest Marriott. She literally assembled her own bed-and-breakfast. You can tell that her creative wheels had already been spinning when she brought the idea up to her husband, because she specifically mentioned the penthouse design and what she would put in the room: a bed, a table, a chair, and a lamp.

Notice these items are in every modern hotel room. This woman was thinking way ahead of her time. Some of my favorite hotel rooms put such incredible creativity and thought into the space. There's an obvious heart for the room to be a retreat, a place of rest. This woman used her designing talents, resources, and time to offer Elisha an inviting atmosphere of rest.

We can do the same thing today in our homes, families, communities, schools, and workplaces. No matter what's going on in our lives, we can sow kindness and generosity. We can pour into others instead of retreating into our busy schedules and even our pain.

We find out later in 2 Kings 4 that this notable woman didn't have a son, and her husband was old. As we've already studied from two women in the Bible, the ache of this longing is such a real struggle. Still, this woman served others in her pain—flourishing and inspiring living at its finest.

When we're in pain, one of the best ways we can create space for others is to tell our stories. Years ago, I read a book about how to style your home. One chapter's subtitle stood out to me: "Your Home, Your Story." The author talked about how our homes should tell a story. The velvet chair in the corner, the shag rug under the coffee table, the antique mirror perfectly placed on the entryway table—the objects should share the reason for their being. A memory. A sentiment. A passion.

Story is king, as the saying goes. And if we are to help people, part of that means being storytellers. From the time Lenya went home to heaven, we have allowed God to use the pain attached to our story. While it has been an honor to witness countless lives changed, it can sometimes be difficult to be the "grief experts" helping others walk through their sorrow. To be honest, there have been times when I haven't wanted to put myself out there and take a phone call or pray with someone in person so I wouldn't have to revisit my pain. Pretty selfish, right? But I have to fight to be the carrier of the story God has allowed us to have. It's a privilege to be trusted with this pain. So many people walk through similar journeys, but they don't get the honor of sharing it with thousands upon thousands of people.

A friend once told us that even though we will be known as experts in this kind of pain, it's okay and expected to still grieve, with others and alone. If God has called us to tell our story, He will continue to strengthen us in the journey. But as much as we may want to crawl in a hole and keep the pain to ourselves, we can't stay there forever. When we trust God, He can do remarkable things in our lives and in the lives of those around us as we share our stories.

We can be the strong, notable women we were created to be as we strengthen each other with the stories of God's faithfulness and grace.

What to Pray When You Don't Know What to Do

On July 15, 2017, our son, Lennox Alexander Lusko, entered the world. God gave us this gift of a little man whom we didn't know would change us and our lives so wonderfully. Levi and I thought we were going to be parents to four daughters, and we were totally happy about it. It's crazy to think that if Lenya were still with us, we probably wouldn't have our only son. Levi was scheduled to get the surgery (you know the one), but after Lenya went to heaven, we cancelled that appointment, not sure of what we were going to do.

Fast forward five years, and we were finally a family free of diapers, diaper bags, toddler beds, baby swings, and pack 'n plays. You name it, we had given it away. In October 2016, Levi and I were in Johannesburg, South Africa. I had bought these amazing high-waisted gray jeans to wear on this trip. As I put them on, I was shocked to discover they didn't fit the way they had when I had tried them on a few weeks prior. What was going on? Maybe I was eating too much South African dessert.

One night I couldn't sleep; jet lag was hitting me hard. Levi was sleeping peacefully, as he always does, even far from home. I didn't want to wake him, so I went into the bathroom of our hotel room, put some blankets and pillows in the bathtub, and laid down in there with my Bible. I know, it's weird now that I'm writing it out. But a jet-lagged girl's gotta do what a jet-lagged girl's gotta do.

That night I read the Word and prayed something to the effect of *God, I'm ready for whatever you have for me because I know you will lead me in what is best.* I felt God speaking to my heart to get ready for a new season. Little did I know that I was already pregnant with our son, and that new season would take us back to Babyland, Diaper World, and Not-a-Lot-of-Sleepville.

It was a hard season because I didn't want to be pregnant again. It was not in our plan, but it was always in God's plan, and for that I'm so very grateful. After Lennox was born, I wrote this in my journal on August 16, 2017:

This recovery has been dang painful. Right now, Lennox is one month old, and my nipples still hurt, my cramps have been ridiculously painful, and my neck went out today. Lennox is doing really well, but sheesh, I'm hurting. Trying to see the purpose in this pain, trying to get the most out of it and not let it be wasted as silly as this pain seems.

Lord, help me see this the way You do. Help me be loving and kind in the midst of pain.

I also just realized why I've been extra cautious this time with #5. I knew this, but it didn't connect till last night while I was in the shower. Yes, I've had Daisy and Clover since Lenya was born, but I've never had a baby born since Lenya died. Hard. Lord, I trust You.

I had never been in this situation before. I had never experienced the joy of having a baby while the shadow of death and grief loomed in the distance. It was like building up a new muscle of trusting God. That's what fighting to live this life of faith is all about: walking through the new and the old while holding on tightly to Jesus. I'm reminded of what the Bible says in 2 Chronicles 20:12, when God's people were heading into a battle but they didn't know what to do next. Their leader, a guy named Jehoshaphat, prayed, "O our God, will You not judge them? For we have no power against this great multitude that is coming against us; nor do we know what to do, but our eyes are upon You."

I love that the reference for this verse is 20:12 because 2012 was a joyous year and also the hardest year for us, with Clover's birth and Lenya's death. There's so much strength in a prayer like that: "We don't know what to do, but our eyes are on You." We are helpless on our own, but we can be filled with hope because God is with us.

Make the Most of It

I believe that the best way to show up and stand out—even when you're facing the unknown—is to make the most of your circumstances, particularly your pain. It's the same principle as when you work out: you receive the most benefit when you engage your whole body. For instance, if you focus on engaging your core when you run, you'll not only be trimming your legs and tightening your rear; you'll also be firming your abs. Multitasking at its finest! The idea is that it's efficient and better for you to make the most of your movements.

A few years back I took an early-morning SoulCycle class. At the beginning of the workout the instructor said, "Make sure you didn't get up this early only to halfway show up." She meant that if we made the effort to sign up and pay for the class, if we made the effort to get up before dawn and grab an Uber to the studio, why would we invest only a little effort into the workout? The only way to get the most out of it is to put the most into it.

How can we get the most out of the movement God has for our lives—this moment, this trial, this heartache, this loss, this process? Levi once said, "It is a great honor to be entrusted with pain. Let it be a passport that will take you to places you could never go before." Show up in the middle of the pain and see how God might want to use you in your struggle. Ask Him, "God, what do you have for me in this?"

Levi's book *Through the Eyes of a Lion* was published in August 2015, a little more than two and a half years after Lenya went to heaven. We decided we wanted to bring copies of the book, along with cookies and balloons, to the hospital where Lenya had been taken.

With permission from the hospital administration, we proceeded to take the daunting steps into the same building that we hadn't set foot in since December 20, 2012. Levi and I walked in with Alivia, who was nine, and Daisy, who was five. I carried Clover, who was three. I couldn't stop the tears from falling down my face. We walked through the same doors where we walked out two and a half years earlier without our Lenya. My heart pounded in my chest as memories from that cold night flashed through my mind.

When we approached the front desk, Levi said something like, "We were in here almost three years ago when our daughter went to heaven. We are so thankful for your staff that worked that night. We wanted to give you the book that came out as a result of what happened."

I'm not sure anyone knew how to react. Some of the staff members just stared at us. Others were thankful, offering us their condolences.

It was a hard moment, yet so healing. If your heart is to let God grow and change you, He can use you in the most difficult of moments to bring help and healing to others.

Jesus showed us this. In Matthew 14, we read how His cousin and close friend, John, was murdered. The disciples took John's body, buried it, and then went to tell Jesus. What did Jesus do? He departed by boat to a deserted place (vv. 12–13). He needed to grieve, and process, and pray—alone. This is a great example to follow. Get away from the crowd. Go somewhere by yourself. Bring your pain and your disappointed, frustrated, or broken heart to God.

But Jesus didn't stay alone; a crew of people followed him. Even in His pain, Jesus didn't stop them and tell them to leave Him alone. He had compassion for them. He hurt, but He was willing to heal. He grieved, but He recognized that the people needed a touch from God. He chose to bring good to others even though He was in pain Himself. And this was when Jesus took five loaves of bread and two fish and fed more than five thousand people (vv. 19–20). Although He was grieving, He used it as a catalyst to His giving.

Making the most out of your struggle is not just possible; it's actually God's best plan for you. In 1 Peter, the author wrote to a local church that was struggling: "In this you greatly rejoice, though now for a little while, if need be, you have been grieved by various trials, that the genuineness of your faith, being much more precious than gold that perishes, though it is tested by fire, may be found to praise, honor, and glory at the revelation of Jesus Christ, whom having not seen you love" (1:6–8).

What is the goal of a flourishing life? That the genuineness of our faith would be proved by the trials that grieve us. That we would point to the revelation of Jesus. That we would live now, fueling our fight through the struggle.

What God does in you isn't just for you. As you lean in to front-row living, He wants to not just do the beautifying work in you but to work through you to strengthen those around you. Keep showing up; keep standing out. God is up to something.

What God

does in you

isn't just

for you.

16

Wait, There's More

A few years ago, Daisy and Clover were performing in the kids' version of *The Lion King* in our town. The girls were so excited to be a cheetah and a zebra. They had practiced hard, and when it was time for the dress rehearsal on the night before their performance, they were ready.

The rehearsal was scheduled to start at 4:00 p.m. We got there on time. (Just in case you missed that, we got there *on time*. Small victories, people.) Rehearsal was quickly pushed back to 5:00 p.m. And then to 6:30 p.m. By that point, most of the kids had melted into piles of whiny, tired, and confused little people. They didn't know that the night had only just begun, and the next couple of hours would be full of "hurry up and wait." That's just how rehearsals go, but the kids didn't seem to have gotten the memo.

Once the children had their costumes on, they had to wait quietly backstage until they were called to practice their parts. I mustered up all the enthusiasm and excitement I possibly could and attempted to encourage the weary troops.

"Isn't it so amazing that you guys get to be in this play? I know it's hard to wait and to be quiet and stand still, but tomorrow you're going to be in the actual performance and it's going to be so worth it!" I'm not sure how effective my pep talk was, but it seemed to appease them for at least five minutes.

By 8:30 p.m., the kids were coming and going to rehearse their parts, but the times of waiting in between were pretty rough. Since it was past dinnertime and none of the kids had eaten for a few hours, they were hungry, but they couldn't eat because they were in their costumes. Double whammy. I remember hearing a little girl sigh dramatically and moan, "I don't want to be here!"

With a bigger smile than before, I said, "Hang in there, kids! We're almost there! The show is going to be amazing! It's going to be so much fun!"

At 9:30 p.m., we were still there . . . and still waiting. Lord, help us! The children were sweating in their heavy costumes and complaining that they were too hot. Some could barely stand up because they were falling asleep. I couldn't blame them. I was feeling it too.

With tears in his eyes, a little boy looked up at me and said in his exhaustion, "I don't even know why I wanted to do this. This is so hard."

Time for another rally—and this time, I needed it too. "I know this is so hard. I understand. I'm with you. It's hot. You're hungry. You've been waiting so long. But let's not give up. Don't quit now. You've been working so hard practicing to be in this play, and it's almost here!"

As I watched the children wait and wait, many of them wanting to quit, I couldn't help but think the scene was a fitting picture of what Paul wrote in Galatians 6:9–10.

And let us not grow weary while doing good, for in due season we shall reap if we do not lose heart. Therefore, as we have opportunity, let us do good to all, especially to those who are of the household of faith.

The children hadn't signed up for waiting. They signed up to be in a play. They signed up to have fun and be a part of something amazing. But this part wasn't fun. This was hard and disappointing, and they were the epitome of weary.

Likewise, we sign up to do awesome, awe-inspiring things for God. But when our experiences don't match our expectations—when we're stuck waiting behind a curtain, *not* doing what we thought God told us we were going to go—suddenly we're tired, hot, and hungry.

We signed up to make a difference, be an influence, have a genuine impact in the world. Instead, we find ourselves sitting as a receptionist in a small office, cleaning up after messy people, serving on a team at church doing something that's outside our sweet spot, or immersed in seemingly insignificant daily tasks that offer little to no recognition. We feel as though the gifts and talents and skills we were born with are not being used but rather are wasting away. Then we see the fun, glamorous, and exciting stuff happening to other people through pics on Instagram, filtered through apps that make everyone look tan, blemish-free, slender, and as happy as if they just won the lottery.

Enter our whiny objections:

"Why am I even here?"

"I'm not doing what makes me happy."

"Where did I go wrong?"

"I don't want to be here with these people."

"I don't want to do this anymore."

It's easy to find yourself in a place where you're wanting to do something else, somewhere else, with someone else. But wait a second. Stop right there. Going any farther down this road will lead you directly to "if only." It's a trap. And it's a dangerous one.

Wherever God has called you to, there will be waiting of some kind. Even if you were to follow the seemingly better option, there would be waiting there too. Starting fresh somewhere else or with someone else won't be as easy as you think.

So stay where you are and don't rush the process. Don't try to get the SparkNotes edition of your life or the FastPass through the difficulty. There's no pushing past the growth of a seed. You just have to wait.

A garden endures different seasons, and each year looks different. Some winters are harsh. Some springs are dry. One year may produce bigger dahlias and a higher yield of tomatoes than the last.

Likewise, our growth looks different every season. We can't expect the blooming will be exactly the same every time. This is the beauty of trusting God in this season, right here and right now. Maybe the growth in your life won't ever look like it does now, in this season that you're in. And I know from my own experience, it won't always feel like it does now.

Jesus came to earth so that we may have life and have it more abundantly (John 10:10). That's His heart for us—abundant living. But it's so easy to give up when it gets hard. The temptation to want to disengage or opt out can be really strong, but those are the moments when—though you can't see it—God is at work.

In the process of writing this book, I've wanted to quit at least twenty times because it has seemed impossible. But as I showed up, opened my laptop and my Bible, cried it out, and just started typing, very slowly the words came. God gave me strength in the struggle—and my husband and kids and friends cheering me on in the background. He will do the same for you. He will provide. God will bring a breakthrough. In the words of Rocky Balboa, "Going in one more round when you don't think you can. That's what makes all the difference in your life."

Just wait, dear heart—there's more.

Life Lessons in the Laundry Room

Laundry. The feelings that this word can evoke are far and wide. Even now, I get a little anxious and exhausted just thinking about the mountains of clothes—dirty *and* clean—waiting for me at home. At this moment, I have a load I put in the wash early this morning, but I haven't had a chance to move it to the dryer, so I'll need to wash the load again to avoid the mildew smell. Sigh.

The other day I did laundry with Lennox. (Yes, doing laundry with a two-year-old might seem like an oxymoron, but I keep him close to me because he is in the stage of running and climbing and getting into spaces he does not need to be in, like the knife drawer. I'm guessing boys never grow out of that stage.) I'd give him a handful of clean, wet clothes from the washer, and he'd place them into the dryer. Eager to help, he kept grabbing more and more. Then, thinking he was done, Lennox shut the dryer door.

"Wait, sweetie. There's more," I said. We opened the door back up, and Lennox took more wet clothes from my hand and threw them into the dryer. He shut the door again and ran away.

"Wait, Lennox," I called out. "There's more, buddy! You can't leave yet. You gotta wait. There's actually more!" I ran after him and caught him before he bolted into the bathroom to unroll the toilet paper.

We finished the load together. (Okay, I did it.) Isn't that the truth, though—there's always more laundry? It seems impossible to ever catch up. Even when every piece of laundry is washed, dried, folded, and put away, there will always be more. In this sense, laundry is a dreaded thing that awaits us all. But what God has been speaking to me is that if we could just wait out the trials of life, hold on for a little bit longer, we'd see that He has so much more for us.

When you're losing heart, when you feel like giving up, when the season you're in doesn't make sense, just wait. There's more. When it seems you're losing the fight, breathe, towel off, hydrate, lean in, and learn all you can. Keep fighting. Keep giving it all you've got. God promises that there is more.

The Greatest More There Is

I love being able to travel and visit different cities and meet so many incredible people. While my favorite part is coming home, every time I return from a trip, I feel an underlying tension.

> *February 21, 2014*
> *428 days*
>
> *Coming home from trips is hard, because it's always good to come home, but coming home never fulfills the ache we have of really coming HOME. And every time we get back, it reminds me that this isn't our real home. Heaven is home.*

In the midst of the struggle, in the midst of the waiting and working, we've got to remember the ultimate *more*. I mentioned Hebrews 11 when we were talking about Sarah. Check out that whole chapter when you get a minute; it's awe inspiring. It shares the importance of something we can't forget in this life as we fight to flourish—the spiritual giants who lived before us. These people believed God, lived for Him, sought to please Him, obeyed Him, and loved Him. Here's part of that chapter:

> These all died in faith, not having received the promises, but having seen them afar off were assured of them, embraced them and confessed that they were strangers and pilgrims on the earth. For those who say such things declare plainly that they seek a homeland. And truly if they had called to mind that country from which they had come out, they would have had opportunity to return. But now they desire a better, that is, a heavenly country. Therefore God is not ashamed to be called their God, for He has prepared a city for them. (Hebrews 11:13–16)

Wait—these heroes died *before* they received the promises? They worked hard, they waited, they believed God, they waited some more . . . and then they died? What the heck? They didn't even receive the fullness of what He promised them. *God, how could You? You led them on!* These men and women saw God's promises from far away. They believed, died, and are now part of the cloud of witnesses mentioned in Hebrews 12, cheering us on to keep running. Can you imagine?

Heaven is the biggest *more* there is. We may not ever see with our own eyes God's answers to our prayers in the way we expected. We may never experience the healing we asked for in this life. We may never get to see our kids flourish in their own walks with God. But God is working more deeply than we can see. And this earth, this life, isn't all there is. There's more—the *real* more. Our homeland. Our heavenly country. That's the real thing.

This earth,

this life, isn't

all there is.

There's more—

the *real* more.

Joni Eareckson Tada is a gem of a human. When she was seventeen, she broke her neck in a diving accident and became a paraplegic. Joni is a beautiful example of a woman who honors God with her story and her limitations—limitations she doesn't let hinder her or her purpose. She won't experience life on earth without a wheelchair, but she knows there is so much more for her around the corner. Joni doesn't know how much time she has left, but she does know that her greatest *more* is coming. Until then, she will tell of God's great love and purpose and will continue to empower kids with disabilities through her Joni and Friends ministry. Joni knows she's passing through this world and is a pilgrim, but she is working with all her heart to do all that God has for her until He decides to call her home. That's true beauty right there!

One of her books, *Heaven: Your Real Home*, brought me great hope and peace in the days after Lenya went to heaven. Joni wrote about the dreams she's had in which God has shown her how in her real home, in heaven, she'll be able to walk and swim and dance. I particularly love this part:

Everything in heaven will have more substance than we ever dreamed. . . . We will no longer desire our God who is absent, but rejoice in our God who is present.

Heaven is being with Jesus. It's not a place where short, chubby, naked baby angels strum tiny harps on clouds or where we sing hymns all day on long, hard pews. It's a place of perfection where we will enjoy the real, abundant life we were made for, a place without sin, shame, pain, tears, trouble, darkness, or grief. I don't know every detail about heaven, but I do know it will be more than we can even dream of or imagine.

Whatever pleasures await us in heaven, I know that God is preparing a place for those who know and love Jesus. I know it will be good; just think of what He created in seven days at the beginning of time!

We're in the waiting now. We're already walking in the promises of God as He is changing us and making us more like Jesus, but we're not fully there yet. The Bible says we're a new creation in Christ, but we're not a perfectly new creation yet. We can flourish now, but we're also fighting forward and we won't be perfectly flourished until heaven.

I still have a Lenya-shaped hole in my heart, and I know I will see her again, just not yet. I have the hope of heaven, but the truth of eternal life then doesn't remove the ache of not having her here with me now; it just cradles it with hope. A little over a year after she died, I wrote:

Oh sweet Lenya, how I miss you, beauty girl. Your laugh, your voice, your hugs, your snuggles, your tenderness, your joy, sassiness, roughness, diet, hands and feet, messy hair, beautiful eyes, gymnast body, love, excitement + enthusiasm, how you looked at your Daddy + cared for your sisters. I wish I could hug you NOW, but I can't wait for that day.

This ache and the yearning for more—for the day of reunion, for the day when we won't have to ever say goodbye again—is meant to lead us home.

A Crowd in Your Corner

Until the day Christ calls us home to heaven for good, take heart and lean in to the heroes who have gone before us:

This ache and

the yearning

for more is

meant to lead

us home.

> Therefore we also, since we are surrounded by so great a cloud of witnesses, let us lay aside every weight, and the sin which so easily ensnares us, and let us run with endurance the race that is set before us, looking unto Jesus, the author and finisher of our faith, who for the joy that was set before Him endured the cross, despising the shame, and has sat down at the right hand of the throne of God. (Hebrews 12:1–2)

We're supported by a solid crew of people who have already died, who are already in the presence of God. They have finished their races. They see the end from the beginning. They have the true perspective now.

I want to take a moment to soak in these verses and go through them more in depth. These truths from God's Word can transform your life as you engage in the struggle to cultivate the life you were born to live.

"Since we are surrounded by so great a cloud of witnesses." In Greek, the word *cloud* means "a dense crowd." The word *witnesses* speaks of an "eye- or ear-witness . . . approaches the . . . sense of martyr," which is someone "who gives public testimony to his faith before a tribunal, and suffers the penalty." This cloud of witnesses suffered in some way for their faith. Maybe they didn't all die as martyrs, but they died believing in Jesus and suffering through life in some way. Now they're cheering us on in our own races. We've got a dense crowd in our corner telling us that if they made it, we can too.

"Let us lay aside every weight, and the sin which so easily ensnares us." *Weight* speaks of a burden. *Sin* means "error, a wrong state of mind or soul." Before we run, we've got to cast aside the things that hold us back. Imagine taking a boxing class and, instead of putting on standard-issue lightweight gloves, you fitted your hands with ones that weighed fifty pounds. You'd struggle to even lift your hands, let alone land a punch. What holds you back that you can stand to get rid of?

"Let us run with endurance." Regardless of how we feel about running, it's what we're all called to. I told you earlier I was a good sprinter in high school, but when it came to long-distance, I'd hit the wall every time and crawl my way to the finish line. But God calls us to run with endurance—to withstand pain, trusting Jesus to the very end, even if our sides are cramped up and our legs are on fire.

"The race that is set before us." This is the part that struck me the most. The Greek word for race is *agón*, which looks deceiving, as if it's the Greek version of the English word *agony*. It's not; it means "an (athletic) contest; a struggle (in the soul)." We're called to run with endurance the athletic contest and the struggle that is set before us. Not just sometimes, either; this is how we're meant to live.

"Set before" speaks to already being placed. It means "I am set (placed or put) before, I am already there." Christ has already made the way to the finish line—to heaven, to living perfectly pure in His presence—for us. If we choose to believe in Him, we've already won; we can then work out of a place of flourishing that already marks our lives.

When you're weary and questioning, like the kids who wondered why they'd signed up for the play in the first place, remember you are flourishing right now. You are! You've got people here on earth and in heaven who are in your corner, cheering you on. And don't ever forget your greatest Fan, Friend, and Coach: Jesus. He sits you down on the stool in the corner of the ring, cups your sweaty and battered face with His hands, looks you in the eyes, and tells you, "Keep fighting. Don't quit. Keep going. Just wait—there's more." And when you can barely lift up your gloved hands to protect yourself, He fights for you.

17

God Fights for You

Recently, Levi and I were having dinner at a restaurant with another couple. Our waitress had a beautiful accent. When we asked, she told us she was from Romania. Levi spent a month on a mission trip there when he was fourteen, and he still remembered a few phrases in Romanian. Without skipping a beat, he told the waitress, *"Iisus te iubeste"*—"Jesus loves you."

Not knowing a thing about her, Levi didn't know how she would respond. But her whole countenance lit up. Smiling wide, she nodded and immediately replied, "Oh yes, I'm His favorite."

I had never heard that said before. *I am God's favorite.* I was hit by this young woman's confidence in God's love for her. She didn't just think she was His favorite; she *knew*. The interaction left a mark on me, and I left the restaurant that night feeling like God had spoken just to me.

You're My favorite, sweetheart.

He speaks this to you, too, but it's something you have to realize on your own. People can tell you over and over how special you are, but it's something you have to believe about yourself. Throughout

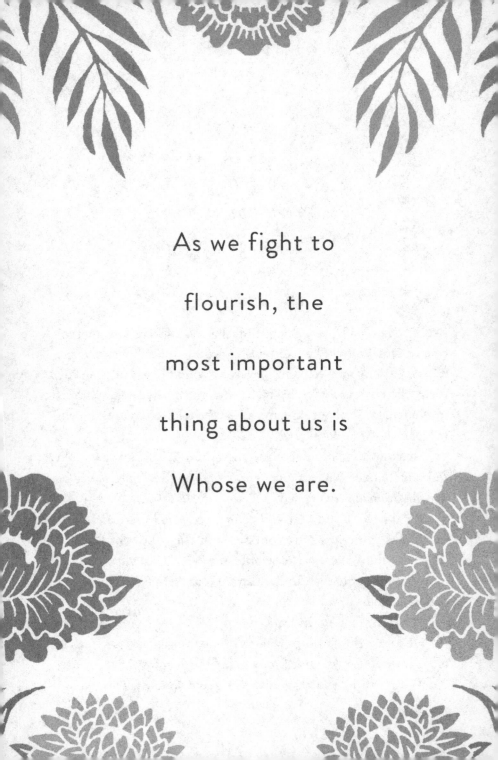

As we fight to

flourish, the

most important

thing about us is

Whose we are.

my life, I've heard people tell me that I am special to God, that I am loved and chosen and called and precious. I'm so thankful for the people who have spoken such generous words over me, but these truths didn't mean as much until I knew them for myself.

As we fight to flourish, the most important thing about us is Whose we are.

So often our lives are ruled by fear. We may fear that we'll get to the end of our lives and find out we got it all wrong. We may fear that we're failing the people we love the most. We may fear that God doesn't really love us. These are the fears that weigh me down when I'm overwhelmed and obsessed with my failures. Walking confidently in His love, however, brings freedom. To believe and know and say "I am His favorite" is a hack to living flourishingly.

This isn't always easy for me. I can't tell you how many times, especially since Lenya died, that I have said, "This is hard. I hate this struggle. I wish I wasn't in this fight right now. I want easy." As I was reading through my pile of journals while writing this book, I came across one that reminded me to flip my focus away from my fears and zero in on what God was calling me to do right now.

February 11, 2013
53 days

"And God will wipe away every tear from their eyes; there shall be no more death, nor sorrow, nor crying. There shall be no more pain, for the former things have passed away" (Revelation 21:4).

Jesus defeated the power of death. But on THIS day, death will die. Today:
• Have confidence in Christ.

- *Walk close to Jesus.*
- *Don't let anything be wasted.*
- *Be a good wife.*
- *Be a fun mom.*
- *Take your role seriously, but not yourself.*

Lord, have Your way in me today. Open my eyes to see how You see.

When I get sucked into a vortex of grief or pain or confusion or doubt, I have to remind myself that not only does God love me and I'm His favorite, but He also knows me best because He created me. For whatever reason—which I may not know until heaven—God has allowed these challenges into my life. So I embrace my situation and engage my life in a way that points others to the Savior who loves us.

The True Heavyweight Champion

As you build your confidence in Christ's love for you, remember that you're not doing it alone. A gardener can cultivate the soil, plant the seeds, and water them, but she can't make them grow. The same is true for you and me. God is at work in the unseen, producing what we cannot produce on our own. Until we absorb the power that only comes from God through the Holy Spirit in Christ Jesus, we'll remain seeds that do not germinate. We will become the picture on the seed packet only if we lean into His power.

When we choose to follow Jesus, we inherit the power of God. In a boxing match, a fighter's coach is able to be in the ring with his boxer only when the boxer is not fighting. But in life, God is always with us, giving us Captain Marvel–style punches. Not only does he empower us to keep showing up and building our endurance but He is also strong in our weakness.

The Bible is full of instances where God shows up and fights for His people. In Exodus 14 we find Moses—the guy who asked God to send someone else to lead the Israelites—leading God's people away from their enemies and toward the Red Sea. Way to grow, Moses!

This was a huge undertaking. Moses had to lead a few million people—without boats or flotation devices and with a ton of luggage—across a sea that at its widest part spanned 220 miles. And hot on their heels were Pharaoh and his army: six hundred soldiers from special ops teams on chariots, all fueled with vengeance.

This chain of events understandably freaked out the Israelites. They had been suddenly removed from the only life they had known and plunged into a new one full of uncertainty and heat and hunger and thirst and lots of danger.

Moses took charge: "Do not be afraid. Stand still, and see the salvation of the LORD, which He will accomplish for you today. For the Egyptians whom you see today, you shall see again no more forever. The LORD will fight for you, and you shall hold your peace" (Exodus 14:13–14). In other words, "It's okay, kids. Don't be scared. Our God will fight for us." That's our God, our ultimate heavyweight champion of all time.

Moses didn't know how God was going to deliver them. This is the life of a true leader—rallying the troops, leading the way from a place of faith, but then whispering to God, "Okay, so how exactly are You going to do this?" It was only *after* Moses assured the people that God gave Moses the battle strategy and showed up in the way that only God can.

"But lift up your rod, and stretch out your hand over the sea and divide it. And the children of Israel shall go on dry ground through the midst of the sea." (Exodus 14:16)

If we look at this situation with human eyes, the battle was impossible for the Israelites to win. But not for God: He split the sea so His children could cross, then made the waters crash down and drown Pharaoh and his army when they tried to follow. This story reminds me to trust my God, because whatever the fight, He's got it.

I'm fascinated by the role Moses and the Israelites played in this story. First, Moses told the people to not be afraid, to stand still, and to see. Then God told Moses to lift up his rod, stretch out his hand over the sea, and divide it. Finally, Moses told the people to go. That's it. Those were the only instructions in this situation. Oh, and they had to believe and trust God, which is usually the hardest part.

What an example for us to look to as we wrap up our time together. God loves you. He cares for you. He is with you. He will fight for you. Your part? Believe Him. Trust Him. Keep your hands up in surrender, and just keep walking. When you come up against the impossible, when you feel like you're losing the fight, when you're so weary you can't lift your fists to protect yourself, look up. See that God is there, and watch Him fight for you.

The Rose in Your Corner

While driving through the winding roads of Sonoma County, California, through charming towns and sprawling vineyards, I noticed that at the end of almost every row of vines was a rose bush. I asked our friend who is a vineyard operator about it. He told us

Believe Him.

Trust Him. Keep

your hands up in

surrender, and just

keep walking.

that the rose bushes act like an early warning system. If there is a problem, such as a disease or a bug infestation, the rose bush will show it first. For example, one of the biggest threats to vineyards in California is a powdery mildew called *oidium*. The rose bush is more susceptible to this mildew, so when it shows up on the roses, the vineyard workers spray a sulfur on the vines that saves them from what could have taken them out. The rose bushes defend the grapes so they stay healthy and flourish and ultimately produce the bottles of wine that appear on dinner tables or at parties.

I don't know a better symbol to end with than the rose.

The rose of Sharon, believed to be a prophetic symbol for Jesus, first appears in Scripture in Song of Solomon 2:1. Isaiah 33:9 also mentions it, describing Sharon as a place, a wilderness. To say that Jesus is our rose in the wilderness is a beautiful illustration of our Savior.

Charles Spurgeon expressed this idea perfectly:

> Whatever there may be of beauty in the material world, Jesus Christ possesses all that in the spiritual world in a tenfold degree. Amongst flowers the rose is deemed the sweetest, but Jesus is infinitely more beautiful in the garden of the soul than the rose can in the gardens of earth. . . . "I am the rose of Sharon." This was the best and rarest of roses. Jesus is not "the rose" alone, He is "the rose of Sharon," just as He calls His righteousness "gold," and then adds, "the gold of Ophir"—the best of the best. He is positively lovely, and superlatively the loveliest.

We read in the previous chapter that Jesus is the author and finisher of our faith (Hebrews 12:2), the answer to our ache within, the One who builds, heals, and restores, the best of the best. Jesus is the rare, precious rose of all creation. His body died on the cross, absorbed our sin—the weight that easily entangles us—and rose up triumphantly from the grave, defeating death and its power. He has given us everything we need to shed our old ways and to flourish until we see Him face-to-face in heaven.

The power isn't ours to muster up or figure out; the power is in Christ, the One who rose up on the cross to die and who rose to live forever.

This is the hope I hold on to, knowing my rose of a Lenya lion is with *the* Rose of all creation. And this same invincibility and hope and peace is for you to hold on to.

Take a look in the mirror. Go ahead, bring me with you. The ingredients for a fresh and flourishing life are right in front of you: you, your circumstances, your struggle. Your Savior, the hope of glory. You don't have to have it all together for God to work in you. He just wants *you*. You're His favorite. And with Him, the Rose who already took on your guilt and shame and struggle and pain, you can face the fight. You are becoming more and more each day like the picture on the seed packet: Jesus.

Our failures may be many, our lives wrought with starts and stops, but we're growing in that soil of struggle. So strap on your wrist wraps, put on your gloves, step into the ring, and with the power and protection of God, face this moment, this day, this life. Embrace your weakness. Let God fight for you. I believe with all my heart that you will flourish.

Acknowledgments

(Because There's No Way I Could've Done This All by Myself)

Thank You, God, for the privilege and heartache of writing this book. Thank You for making me do the hard things; You do all things well.

Levi, you push me to fight through the struggle more than anyone. You have seen me on my worst days and best days and everything in between, and yet you adore me and believe in me. Thank you for telling me I could write when I thought I couldn't and that this process wouldn't kill me when I thought it would. You are so special to me; I'm stronger because of you.

AJ, you are a beautiful person with a true gift of writing and of encouragement. You not only helped me do one of the hardest things of my life, but many times your texts and emails gave me the love and strength and jolt I needed in the moment to take the next hard step. You are a gift to me. Thank you for doing the impossible with me and making it fun!

Esther, none of this would have happened if you hadn't stopped me and told me you thought I should write a book. Thank you for working hard to make this happen, for your kindness and encouragement, *and* for helping Levi find his ring.

Lysa, the way you share what God has gifted you with is such a precious thing. Thank you for helping me, for helping my team, for being so willing to share the secret sauce.

Joel, thank you for your incredible Bible knowledge and willingness to help me uncover some of the most beautiful truths.

Meaghan, you are a magician, plain and simple. You are a beautiful soul who takes each task and job with all your heart. It's really been a joy to work with you. Thank you for helping me take this to the next level.

Debbie, you have been on this journey with us as a family from the very start, and from day one you have been such a constant voice of love and care and courage. I am grateful for you in my life.

To the whole W Publishing team: I'm so thankful for each and every one of you working so hard to make this book a reality. Thank you for being the best team.

To the whole Fedd Agency team: Thank you for your love and diligence and care. Love you all!

Daisy Hutton, I'm so thankful for your part in the process. It was short and sweet and so appreciated.

Elisha Lynn, you are a wizard. A wonderful wizard. Thank you for pouring your heart and soul into not only the art but into the heart of this book. Thank you for your strength and grace and for the seed packet. Girl!

Katelyn, you are a gem, and your creativity and vision is golden. Thank you for your perspective and for your heart and boldness and excellence in taking things I say and do to the next level. I love you.

Alie Gwinn, you are a special one, and everything you touch

turns to gold. Thank you for your words of wisdom and encouragement throughout this whole process. Thank you for being there when I just needed someone to look me in the eyes and say, "That's really good, Jennie!" I'm better because of you.

Mckenzie, thank you for being the steady one behind the scenes, helping me schedule, and plan, and meet, and do all the things I would otherwise forget or not know how to do. I love you, and I appreciate you more than words can say.

Holly Furtick, you amaze me all the time. You're the kind of 9 I want to be. You inspire me to be a kind and giving friend. You may not be the best recommender of birth control, but you shine in every other way. I love you!

Mom, thank you for being my friend and for always encouraging me to do what God's called me to. Thank you also for being such a good grandma. I'm so thankful that Lenya knew you and spent so much time with you. I love you, Mom.

Alaina, near or far, you are a source of strength for me. Thank you for your love and your graceful words that always are timely. I love you.

To my Fresh Life family: I can't believe I get to be a part of such a gorgeous and gifted and generous group who are so happy to be a brick in the house and to build what God is building. Love you, church!

Alivia Sky, you are brave. You are strong. God uses you daily in my life in such a special way, and I'm honored to be your mom, and more and more your friend. I love that you were Len's best friend. You have a depth that is rare and precious, and God has a unique plan for you.

Daisy Grace, you are so sweet and strong. Right after Lenya went to heaven, you were the one always by my side and were usually there when I would cry. Your face looking up at me with concern and care is one I'll always carry with me. I'm sorry you had to grow up with sad parents, but my prayer is that you also remember the joy.

Clover Dawn, I love that Lenya held you the day you were born, and that we have videos and pictures of you two together. Your heart and drive and sass remind us of her, but Clover, you are special, tender, and full of life, and God is going to use you powerfully in your future and right now.

Lennox Alexander, you are a joy, son. You brighten our lives, and I can't believe I get to be your mom. Although you won't meet Lenya until heaven, I hope you'll always know her from the stories, from our family silliness, from your wildness, from the fact that she's waiting for us until that day.

Stacia, Victoria, Jael, Schaelen, Jordyn, Olivia, thank you for helping me take care of my kids throughout this whole process. I literally couldn't have done this without you loving and caring for the ones I love the most.

And to all I couldn't mention—because let's be honest, in my empathy/includer ways I could just keep going—thank you all! I love you!

Notes

Introduction

xix **The word *flourish* in Hebrew is *parach*:** Bible Hub, s.v. "6524: Parach," accessed October 9, 2019, https://biblehub.com/str/hebrew /6524.htm.

xxii **This word *fight* in the Greek language:** This definition was accessed via the Logos Bible app, available for download via logos.com.

xxvi **"We had better love with abandon":** Richard Swenson, *In Search of Balance: Keys to a Stable Life* (Colorado Springs, CO: NavPress, 2010), 79.

Chapter 2: Born to Shine

18 **The Hebrew word for "create":** Bible Study Tools, s.v. "*bara*," accessed October 10, 2019, https://www.biblestudytools.com/lexicons /hebrew/nas/bara.html.

19 **The Hebrew word for "good":** Bible Hub, s.v. "*tob*," accessed October 10, 2019, https://biblehub.com/hebrew/2895.htm.

20 **The word *shine* means:** Dictionary.com, s.v. "shine," accessed October 10, 2019, www.dictionary.com/browse/shine.

Chapter 3: Find Your Grit

36 **The Greek word for fight:** *Vine's Greek New Testament Dictionary*, s.v. "*pukteuo*," Gospel Hall, accessed October 10, 2019, http://gospelhall .org/bible/bible.php?search=FIGHT&dict=vine&lang=english.

36 **Another Greek word he used for fight is *agonizomai*:** *Vine's Greek New Testament Dictionary*, s.v. "*agonizomai*," Gospel Hall, accessed October 10, 2019, http://gospelhall.org/bible/bible.php?search=agonizomai&dict=vine&lang=greek#B1.

41 **"When you run from things that scare you":** Levi Lusko, *Through the Eyes of a Lion: Facing Impossible Pain, Finding Incredible Power* (Nashville, TN: W Publishing Group, 2015), 158.

Chapter 4: Keep Your Guard Up

50 **"Her happiness and fulfillment did not depend on her circumstances":** Kristen Burke, "Ruth Bell Graham: 1920–2007," *Decision*, July 24, 2007, https://billygraham.org/decision-magazine/july-august-2007/ruth-bell-graham-1920–2007/.

50 **"She was a spiritual giant":** Billy Graham, "Billy Graham Dies: His Tribute to His Wife, Ruth," *Citizen-Times*, February 21, 2018, https://www.citizen-times.com/story/news/local/2018/02/21/billys-tribute-wife-ruth/110665632/.

54 **We have more access to the Bible in a variety of translations than ever before:** One of my favorite translations is the New International Reader's Version. It puts the language of the Bible in a clear and concise way that my simple mind can understand.

56 **The Hebrew word for hide:** Bible Hub, s.v. "*tsaphan*," accessed October 10, 2019, https://biblehub.com/hebrew/6845.htm.

57 **SOAP:** I first learned about the SOAP method from a blog by Horatio Printing: Polly Payne, "Seasons of Soap," Horatio Printing, January 22, 2018, https://www.horacioprinting.com/blogs/news/seasons-of-soap?_pos=1&_sid=90314ca68&_ss=r.

59 **"Esther twirled her dress in a perfect circle":** It turns out this is actually from Catherine DeVries's *Adventure Bible Storybook* (Grand Rapids, MI: Zonderkidz, 2009), 118.

Chapter 5: Get Back in the Ring

63 **"If you go one more round":** *Rocky IV*, directed by Sylvester Stallone (1985; Los Angeles: 20th Century Fox, 2006), DVD.

73 **"She's tough, I can't go inside":** *Million Dollar Baby*, directed by Clint Eastwood (2004; Burbank, CA: Warner Home Video, 2005), DVD.

Chapter 6: Stick to the Plan

78 **"The turbulence we face":** Charlotte Gambill, *The Miracle in the Middle* (Nashville, TN: W Publishing, 2015), 51.

81 **"The way you fight, anger's your biggest tool":** *Southpaw*, directed by Antoine Fuqua (New York: Weinstein Company, 2015).

82 **"If I could give men and women":** Drake Baer, "One of America's Most Beloved Authors Just Told Us Her 'Number One Life Hack' for Lasting Relationships," Business Insider, August 26, 2015, https://www.businessinsider.com/brene-browns-biggest-life-hack-is-a -simple-phrase-2015-8.

82 **"All I knew was that I had already scripted":** Brené Brown, *Rising Strong* (New York: Random House, 2017), 18.

86 **"breathing correctly when throwing punches":** William McCoy, "Breathing Techniques for Boxing," The Nest, accessed October 11, 2019, https://woman.thenest.com/breathing-techniques-boxing-6184.html.

Chapter 7: Embrace the Beauty in the Blend

94 **"Suffering is the common denominator":** Laura Thomas, "A Stroke Freed Me to Redefine Beauty," *Christianity Today*, February 2017, https://www.christianitytoday.com/women/2017/february /stroke-freed-me-from-fleeting-beauty.html.

94 **"seat of honor":** Jay and Katherine Wolf, "Hope Heals," video, Fresh Life Church, July 7, 2017, http://www.freshlife.church/messages/message .php?id=787.

Chapter 8: Right Here, Right Now

106 **"To engage means":** Dictionary.com, s.v. "engage," accessed October 11, 2019, https://www.dictionary.com/browse/engage?s=t.

107 **"*immerse*, which means":** Dictionary.com, s.v. "immerse," accessed October 11, 2019, https://www.dictionary.com/browse/immerse.

111 The book's theme: "Epilogue," excerpt from Eugene Peterson, *A*

Long Obedience in the Same Direction, 2nd ed. (Downers Grove, IL: InterVarsity Press, 2000), 202, https://www.ivpress.com/Media/Default /Downloads/Excerpts-and-Samples/Long%20Obedience_2257 _EXCERPT.pdf.

111 **"The essential thing 'in heaven and earth'":** Friedrich Nietzsche, *Beyond Good and Evil* (Global Classics, 2018), 46.

Chapter 9: God, Please Send Someone Else

123 **"God was not angry":** David Guzik, "Study Guide for Exodus 4," Blue Letter Bible, 2013, https://www.blueletterbible.org/Comm/guzik _david/StudyGuide2017-Exd/Exd-4.cfm.

125 **"If you don't love yourself":** Louie Giglio, "The Man/Woman in the Mirror," Relatable: Making Relationships Work, Devotional Day 2, Bible.com, accessed October 11, 2019, https://www.bible.com /reading-plans/2984-relatable-making-relationships-work/day/2.

Chapter 10: You Can't Hug a Porcupine

134 **"This is true humility":** Rick Warren, *The Purpose Driven Life* (Grand Rapids, MI: Zondervan, 2002), 262.

134 **"Humility has the power":** Debra Fileta, *Choosing Marriage* (Eugene, OR: Harvest House, 2018), 24.

Chapter 11: Stir Up the Sweetness

146 **"When it comes to your life":** Lance Witt, *High Impact Teams* (Grand Rapids, MI: Baker Books, 2018), 35.

148 **"the word in Greek for 'stir up'":** Bible Hub, s.v. *"paroxusmos,"* accessed October 11, 2019, https://biblehub.com/greek/3948.htm.

148 **"the quality of being intimate and attached":** Dictionary.com, s.v. "warmth," accessed October 11, 2019, https://www.dictionary.com /browse/warmth.

150 **"Just smile and wave, boys":** *Madagascar*, directed by Eric Darnell and Tom McGrath (2005; Universal City, CA: Dreamworks Home Entertainment, 2008), DVD.

155 **I love the word *winsome*:** Dictionary.com, s.v. "winsome," accessed October 11, 2019, https://www.dictionary.com/browse/winsome.

Chapter 12: Stronger Together

164 **a typical friendship lasts about three to five years:** Stasi Eldredge, *Becoming Myself: Embracing God's Dream of You* (Colorado Springs, CO: David C Cook, 2014), 144.

169 **The word *catalyst* means:** Dictionary.com, s.v. "catalyst," accessed November 20, 2019, www.dictionary.com/browse/catalyst.

170 **"besides [her] incredible strength":** Peter Hathaway Capstick, *Death in the Long Grass* (New York: St. Martin's Press, 1977), 110.

170 **A wounded leopard:** Capstick, 146.

Chapter 14: Shake Up the Freshness

192 **"When we come to the place where everything can be predicted":** A.W. Tozer, *Rut, Rot, or Revival* (Chicago: Moody Publishing, 2006), 3, https://www.moodypublishers.com/mpimages/Marketing/web%20Resources/ProductExcerpts/9781600660481-TOC-CH1.pdf.

192 **A rut is:** Dictionary.com, s.v. "rut," accessed October 12, 2019, https://www.dictionary.com/browse/rut.

193 **"Complacency is a deadly foe":** A.W. Tozer, *The Pursuit of God* (Harrisburg, PA: Christian Publications Inc., 2008), eBook location p. 17, http://www.gutenberg.org/files/25141/25141-h/25141-h.htm.

193 **One of the definitions of *fresh*:** Dictionary.com, s.v. "fresh," accessed October 12, 2019, https://www.dictionary.com/browse/fresh.

199 **"Chuck never really cared about being a fighter":** UFC-Ultimate Fighting Championship, "The Ice Age: The Story of Chuck Liddell, the First UFC Superstar," uploaded May 27, 2019, YouTube video, 1:25 and 13:52, https://youtu.be/DherCJxcXCU.

Chapter 15: Show Up and Stand Out

207 **"Do for one what you wish you could do for everyone":** Andy Stanley (@AndyStanley), "Do for one what you wish you could do for everyone," Twitter, March 11, 2019, 5:33 a.m., https://twitter.com/AndyStanley/status/1105084218101641217.

209 **a book about how to style your home:** Kate Watson-Smyth, *Mad About the House: How to Decorate Your Home with Style* (London: Pavilion, 2018).

Chapter 16: Wait, There's More

225 **"Everything in heaven":** Joni Eareckson Tada, *Heaven: Your Real Home* (Grand Rapids, MI: Zondervan, 1996), 80.

228 **In Greek, the word *cloud*:** Bible Hub, s.v. *"nephos,"* accessed November 20, 2019, https://biblehub.com/greek/3509.htm.

228 **The word *witnesses*:** Alexander Souter, *A Pocket Lexicon to the Greek New Testament* (New York: Oxford, 1917), 153.

228 ***Sin* means:** This definition was accessed via the Logos Bible app, available for download via logos.com.

229 **The Greek word for race:** Bible Hub, s.v. *"agón,"* accessed November 20, 2019, https://biblehub.com/greek/73.htm.

Chapter 17: God Fights for You

238 **"Whatever there may be of beauty":** Charles Spurgeon, *Morning and Evening* (Wheaton, IL: Crossway Books, 2003), 102.

About the Author

Jennie Lusko serves alongside her husband, Levi, leading Fresh Life Church in Montana, Utah, Oregon, and Wyoming, as well as across the world online. They have five children: Alivia, Daisy, Clover, Lennox, and Lenya, who is waiting for them in heaven. The Lusko family lives in Montana and enjoys bike rides, walks, lake days, late-night hot tub and cold plunge parties, movies, and family breakfast. Jennie loves spin and boxing, good food and sugary coffee, and wearing the same thing every day but also getting fashion advice from Levi. Jennie is also a hugger, so beware if you meet her.

New Video Study for Your Church or Small Group

If you've enjoyed this book, now you can go deeper with the companion video Bible study!

In this six-session study, Jennie Lusko helps you apply the principles in *The Fight to Flourish* to your life. The study guide includes video notes, group discussion questions, and personal study and reflection materials for in-between sessions.

Study Guide
9780310112488

DVD
9780310112501

Available now at your favorite bookstore, or streaming video on StudyGateway.com.

A PRAYER FOR EVERY SEASON

Do you ever find yourself in a season where you don't know what to pray? Or you're not sure if you even want to pray?

In your free download, step into Jennie's prayer journal by receiving a handwritten word of strength and encouragement that will give you the words to pray through any season.

- A waiting season

- A confusing season

- A challenging season

- A growing season

- A transitioning season

- A suffering season

- A busy season

- A thriving season

Download your handwritten prayers at jennielusko.com/a-prayer-for-every-season

THROUGH THE EYES OF A LION
BY LEVI LUSKO

This can't be real.

These thoughts swim through my mind and try to strangle me. My heart is shattered into a thousand pieces, each shard jagged and razor sharp. The pain is surreal, deafening, and catastrophic. My eyes burn. I want to cry, but the tears won't come. I want to scream, but it won't help. I am afraid. But I'm not alone. . . .

You must not rely on the naked eye. What you think you see is not all that is there. There are unseen things. Spiritual things. Eternal things. You must learn to see life through the eyes of a Lion. Doing so is to utilize the telescope of faith, which will not only allow you to perceive the invisible—it will give you the strength to do the impossible.

—From the introduction.

Through the Eyes of a Lion
will help you:

Embrace the power of hope in a world that is often filled with suffering and loss.

Discover a manifesto for high-octane living when grief and despair are paralyzing.

Learn how to let your pain become your platform.

• • •

LeviLusko.com
Available wherever books and e-books are sold.

Other books available from Levi Lusko include
Swipe Right and *I Declare War*